Selected Poems of
ROBERT FROST

WITH INTRODUCTION BY ROBERT GRAVES

Holt, Rinehart and Winston, Inc.

NEW YORK • CHICAGO • SAN FRANCISCO • ATLANTA • DALLAS
MONTREAL • TORONTO

NOTE

The selection of poems for this volume was made by Mr. Frost, who also made several minor changes in the texts. The title "The Sound of the Trees," as it appears in the *Complete Poems* has been changed to "The Sound of Trees," and "Choose Something Like a Star" has been changed to "Take Something Like a Star." In this edition, Mr. Frost has omitted the last stanza of "Closed for Good." The second stanza of "Peril of Hope" has been slightly changed.

Introduction by Robert Graves copyright © 1963
by International Authors N.V.

Bibliography and biographical note revised by the authors from *Robert Frost: An Introduction* by Robert A. Greenberg and James G. Hepburn copyright © 1961 by Holt, Rinehart and Winston, Inc.

Library of Congress Catalog Card Number: 63-10970

SBN: 03-012060-8

Printed in the United States of America

01234   68   98

Contents

Contents

Contents

A FURTHER RANGE

TAKEN DOUBLY

Contents

Contents

Contents

Introduction by Robert Graves

ROBERT FROST never offends against the decencies by boasting of what he has achieved as a poet. Though he must be well aware that nobody else could have written these poems, which are stamped all over with his own seal, and though plenty of people would give their right hands to have done so, he says simply: 'It's for the world to decide whether you're a poet or not.' The truth is that Frost was the first American who could be honestly reckoned a master-poet by world standards. Poe, Longfellow, Whittier, and many more of his American predecessors had written good provincial verse; and Whitman, a homespun eccentric, had fallen short of the master-poet title only through failing to realize how much more was required of him. Frost has won the title fairly, not by turning his back on ancient European tradition, nor by imitating its successes, but by developing it in a way that at last matches the American climate and the American language.

'Master-poet' has been wrongly read by teachers and college professors who use Frost's work as a ruler to whack on their pupils' knuckles. It means that, like a master-goldsmith or a master-mason, he knows exactly what he is doing and why; not that he is in need of disciples to applaud him. Frost has remarked that being taught poems at school reduces them to the rank of mere information, and that he doubts whether 'poetic literature' deserves a place in the educational curriculum. In other words, poetry should be treated as a private matter. To teach it as class-room literature is like reducing love to public philanthropy, or religion to Church history and doctrine. Nevertheless, most people first become aware of poetry at their schools or colleges; and a few of these, at least, make it a free gift, not a subject for grades.

One good way of judging poets is to pretend that they are still living, even if they have been dead two thousand years or more, and to decide what personal immediacy they still have for you. Imagine yourself saying: 'Tonight there's to be a moonlight barbecue down by the creek. Just ourselves, and maybe two or three special others . . . Would it be fun if John Milton came along? Or Will Shakespeare? Or Johnny Keats? Or Mr. Percy Bysshe Shelley? Or Herr Professor Johann Wolfgang von Goethe? Or Old Homer, the harpist? Or Signor Dante Alighieri?' A quick leaf-through of their poems will give you a pretty shrewd notion which of them would be readily accepted by everyone at the barbecue, including the non-intellectuals, and make you all feel warmer towards each other than before, and perhaps keep an unforgettable conversation going until the small hours. Those special ones would be the master-poets; of whom there have been very few in history.

I agree with Frost that a poem planned beforehand never comes off. Real ones appear unexpectedly, and always at a time when the poet is in a so-called state of grace: which means a clear mind, tense heart, and no worries about fame, money, or other people, but only the excitement of a unique revelation about to be given.

Frost is a quick worker; many of his poems are written straight off. Some, he admits, have trouble in one or two spots that he may never put right, because it is so difficult to recover the trance-like mood in which a poem first entered the mind. A poem's most precious quality, he says, will always be that it ran in from nowhere and carried the poet away with it. Yet sometimes the trouble can be removed, by a sudden insight, twenty or thirty years later.

To understand poetry, a reader must be in the same state of grace as the poet, able to enjoy free play of all his deeper mental and emotional faculties. This calls for concentration, and the poem's printed lay-out is an immediate reminder of this need. That each line begins with a capital letter, and stretches over only a part of the page, draws attention to the metre: which obliges you to give each syllable its full value and proper accent, and to respect the pauses which punctuation demands. Sometimes a poem keeps an even tighter control of your attention by the use of rhyme, alliteration, or other devices.

Frost has always respected metre. When, during the *Vers Libre* period of the Nineteen Twenties and Thirties his poems were disdained as old-fashioned, he remarked disdainfully that writing free verse was like playing tennis without a net. The *Vers Librists*, it should be explained, had rebelled against a degenerate sort of poetry in which nothing mattered except getting the ball neatly over the net. Few games are so wearisome to watch as a methodical ping-pong, ping-pong tennis match in which each player allows his opponent an easy forehand return from the same court. The *Vers Librists*, therefore, abandoned the tennis-net of metre altogether, and concentrated on rhythm. But though metre is boring without rhythm, the reverse is equally true. A rhythmic manipulation of metre means—in this tennis metaphor—so placing your shots that you force the other fellow to dart all round his territory, using backhand, forehand, volley or half-volley as the play demands. Only the 'strain of rhythm upon metre' (Frost's own phrase), makes a poem worth reading, or a long rally in tennis worth watching. That you can't achieve much in poetry without, so to speak, a taut net and straight whitewashed lines, is shown by the difficulty of memorizing free verse; it does not fix itself firmly enough in the imagination.

Frost farmed for ten years among the well-wooded hills of

Vermont. The four natural objects most proper to poems are, by common consent, the moon, water, hills and trees; with sun, birds, beasts and flowers as useful subsidiaries. It is remarkable that, among the ancient Irish, Highland Scots and Welsh, from whose tradition (though at second or third hand) English poetry derives most of its strange magic—the Muse was a Moon, Mountain and Water-goddess, and the word for poetic literature was always 'trees'. Bardic schools were built in forests, not in towns; and every letter of the alphabet had a tree name. Frost's most haunting poems, such as *The Wood-Pile, Birches, An Encounter, Stopping by Woods on a Snowy Evening,* are set in woods. The moon floats above, and water rushes down from every hill. The farmhouse in the clearing— unless it is staging one of those poignant country dramas which are his specialty—provides him with a convenient centre from which to saunter out and commune in thought with the birches, maples, hickories, pines, or wild apples. *Into My Own,* the first poem of Frost's apprentice-work, *A Boy's Will* (1913), begins:

> One of my wishes is that those dark trees,
> So old and firm they scarcely show the breeze,
> Were not, as 'twere, the merest mask of glo m,
> But stretched away unto the edge of doom . . .

Among trees, you are usually alone, but seldom lonely: they are companionable presences for those in love and, although Frost seldom uses the word 'love', all his poems are instinct with it.

He reminds us that poems, like love, begin in surprise, delight and tears, and end in wisdom. Whereas scholars follow projected lines of logic, he collects his knowledge undeliberately, he says, like burrs that stick to your legs when you walk through a field. Surprise always clings to a real poem, however often it is read; but must come naturally, cannot be achieved

by the cunning formula of a short story or detective thriller.
If there have been no tears of surprise in the writer, then there
will be no tears of surprise in the reader. The poetic impulse,
though unforeseeable, can be discouraged all too easily. Most
poets sell themselves to money, religion, literature, politics,
philosophy or social position, before they have reached their
middle 'twenties, and that is the end of them. Frost has never
sold himself, though not shy of mixed company.

One good way of judging a particular poem (once you have
saved time by first judging the poet) is to ask yourself whether
the package contains anything irrelevant to its declared con-
tents, and whether anything essential has been left out. I admit
that even Frost lapses at times into literary references, philosophy, political argument and idle play with words; yet has any
other man now alive written more poems that stand up to this
packaging test? His chief preoccupation is freedom: freedom to
be himself, to make discoveries, to work, to love, and not to be
limited by any power except personal conscience or common·
sense.

One of his best-known poems, *Mending Wall,* begins:

> Something there is that doesn't love a wall,
> That sends the frozen-ground-swell under it,
> And spills the upper boulders in the sun; . . .

He and his neighbour, between them, annually repaired the
wall that separates their farms, each working from his own
side and keeping pace with the other. Although neither of
them raised sheep or cows that might stray into the crops—
Frost had only apple-trees; his neighbour, pines—the repairs
were made to justify the proverb 'Good fences make good
neighbours!' And if anyone asks: 'But what *is* the something
that doesn't love a wall?', the answer is, of course, 'frost'—
also its open-hearted namesake, Robert Frost.

Introduction

The old Vermont way of life ended long ago. Solitude among trees, solitude beside running water or under the moon, fostered these poems. Now the backwoodsman buys himself a television set and finds company enough in the commercials:

> Four-room shack aspiring high
> With an arm of scrawny mast
> For the visions in the sky
> That go blindly pouring past.
> In the ear and in the eye
> 'What you get is what to buy.
> Hope you're satisfied to last.

Though Frost owns to the growing materialism of the United States, which stultifies the Founding Fathers' prayer for courage and self-control among those destined to occupy the land, he refuses to lament bygone times. The land, the tools, and the language are all still available, and he has himself proved how nobly they can be used. Nevertheless, it would be rash to expect that another master-poet of the same quality will appear under the present economic system, despite a shorter working week, improvements in transport, and a greater ease in living. To resist the social pressure now put even on one's leisure time, requires a tougher upbringing and a more obstinate wilfulness about going one's own way, than ever before. A great part of the countryside has been scheduled for industrialization and, as everyone tells me, this is a critical, rather than a creative, age. But give thanks, at least, that you still have Frost's poems; and when you feel the need of solitude, retreat to the companionship of moon, waters, hills and trees. Retreat, he reminds us, should not be confused with escape. And take these poems along for good luck!

R.G.
Deyá, Majorca, Spain.

Robert Frost: A Biographical Note

ROBERT FROST was born on March 26, 1874, in San Francisco, where his father, of firm New Hampshire stock, edited a newspaper. The paper was Democratic and Robert's full name is Robert Lee Frost, two facts which are usually taken to indicate the older Frost's attitude to then-Republican New England. When Robert was eleven, his father died, and he and his schoolteacher mother crossed country and settled with relatives in Massachusetts. His first published poem, on the subject of Cortez in Mexico, appeared in the high school newspaper when he was sixteen. He entered Dartmouth at the age of eighteen, but remained for only about seven weeks. Two years later, in 1895, he married Elinor White, whom he had known in high school. In 1897 he enrolled at Harvard, hoping to prepare for a career in college teaching, but he left after two years without a degree. Frost was then twenty-five.

Disappointed with Frost's erratic progress, his grandfather presented him with a farm in Derry, New Hampshire, on the condition that he retain it for ten years. Farming proved less than profitable, and Frost supplemented his income by teaching school, first at the Pinkerton Academy in Derry and then for a year at the New Hampshire State Normal School in Plymouth, where he taught psychology. Throughout this time he was writing poetry, and though he offered it to various periodicals, very little was printed. When his ten-year obligation at the farm ended, Frost sold the property, and shortly after, in September 1912, he and his family left for England. There he met a number of expatriate American poets, most notably Ezra Pound, but he felt greatest affinity with a group of English poets—Edward Thomas, Lascelles Abercrombie, Wilfred Gibson—who often wrote of rural subjects. Frost's first book of poetry, *A Boy's Will*, consisting largely of what he had written prior to coming to England, was issued in 1913 by an English publisher, who a year later issued Frost's second volume, *North of Boston*. Frost returned to America in 1915 to discover that an American edition of *North of Boston* had recently appeared and that it had provoked a highly favorable response. Later that year *A Boy's Will* also appeared in an American edition.

From this time on, Frost's status as a notable American poet was secure. Though he settled for a time in New Hampshire, and then more permanently in Vermont, he traveled throughout much of the country giving lectures and public readings from his own poetry. His earlier lack of success at Dartmouth and Harvard was more than compensated for by his stints as poet-in-residence at such colleges and universities as Amherst, Harvard, Michigan, and Dartmouth. And he continued to write: in 1916, *Mountain Interval;* in 1923, *New Hampshire;* in 1928, *West-running Brook;* in 1936, *A Further Range;* in 1942, *A Witness Tree;* in 1945, *A Masque of Reason;* in 1947, *Steeple Bush* and *A Masque of Mercy;* in 1962, *In the Clearing.* His public honors have been many: four Pulitzer Prizes for Poetry (1924, 1931, 1937, 1943), innumerable honorary degrees (including ones from Oxford and Cambridge), membership in the National Institute of Arts and Letters (1916) and in the American Academy (1930), the Mark Twain Medal (1937) and the Emerson-Thoreau Medal (1958), the office of Consultant in Poetry to the Library of Congress (1958–1959), and formal felicitations from the United States Senate on his seventy-fifth birthday and then again on his eighty-fifth birthday.

Bibliography

BOOKS BY ROBERT FROST

A Boy's Will, London: Nutt, 1913; New York: Holt, 1915.

North of Boston, London: Nutt, 1914; New York: Holt, 1914.

Mountain Interval, New York: Holt, 1916.

New Hampshire: A Poem with Notes and Grace Notes, New York: Holt, 1923.

Selected Poems, New York: Holt, 1923; revised and enlarged 1928 and 1934.

West-running Brook, New York: Holt, 1928.

Collected Poems, New York: Holt, 1930; reissued in 1939, with Frost's prose preface, "The Figure a Poem Makes."

A Further Range, New York: Holt, 1936.

Selected Poems, London: Cape, 1936; includes introductory essays by W. H. Auden, C. Day Lewis, Paul Engle, and Edwin Muir.

A Witness Tree, New York: Holt, 1942.

A Masque of Reason, New York: Holt, 1945.

The Poems of Robert Frost, New York: Modern Library, 1946; includes Frost's prose preface, "The Constant Symbol."

Steeple Bush, New York: Holt, 1947.

A Masque of Mercy, New York: Holt, 1947.

Complete Poems, New York: Holt, 1949; includes "The Figure a Poem Makes."

In the Clearing, New York: Holt, 1962.

The Letters of Robert Frost to Louis Untermeyer, ed. Louis Untermeyer, New York: Holt, 1963.

BOOKS ON ROBERT FROST

Brower, Reuben A., *The Poetry of Robert Frost: Constellations of Intention*, New York: Oxford University, 1963.

Clymer, W. B. and Charles R. Green, *Robert Frost: A Bibliography*, Amherst, Mass.: The Jones Library, 1937.

Coffin, Robert P. Tristram, *New Poetry of New England: Frost and Robinson*, Baltimore: Johns Hopkins University, 1938.

Cook, Reginald L., *The Dimensions of Robert Frost*, New York: Holt, 1958.

Cox, James Melville, *Robert Frost*, New York: Prentice-Hall, 1962.

Cox, Sidney, *Robert Frost: Original "Ordinary Man,"* New York: Holt, 1929.

———, *A Swinger of Birches: A Portrait of Robert Frost*, New York: New York University, 1957.

Doyle, John Robert, *The Poetry of Robert Frost: An Analysis*, Johannesburg: Witwatersrand University, 1962.

Ford, Caroline, *The Less Traveled Road*, Cambridge: Harvard University, 1935.

Greenberg, Robert A. and James G. Hepburn, *Robert Frost: An Introduction*, New York: Holt, 1961.

Isaacs, Elizabeth, *An Introduction to Robert Frost*, Denver: Alan Swallow, 1962.

Lynen, John F., *The Pastoral Art of Robert Frost*, New Haven: Yale University, 1960.

Mertins, Louis and Esther, *The Intervals of Robert Frost: A*

Critical Bibliography, Berkeley and Los Angeles: University of California, 1947.

Munson, Gorham B., *Robert Frost: A Study in Sensibility and Good Sense,* New York: Doran, 1927.

Nitchie, George W., *Human Values in the Poetry of Robert Frost,* Durham, N. C.: Duke University, 1960.

Sergeant, Elizabeth Shepley, *Robert Frost: The Trial by Existence,* New York: Holt, 1960.

Squires, Radcliffe, *The Major Themes of Robert Frost,* Ann Arbor: University of Michigan, 1963.

Thompson, Lawrance, *Fire and Ice: The Art and Thought of Robert Frost,* New York: Holt, 1942.

———, *Robert Frost,* University of Minnesota Pamphlets on American Writers, No. 2, Minneapolis: University of Minnesota, 1959.

Thornton, Richard, ed., *Recognition of Robert Frost,* New York: Holt, 1937.

ARTICLES AND COMMENTS

Baker, Carlos, "Frost on the Pumpkin," *Georgia Review,* XI (Summer 1957), 117–131.

Beach, Joseph Warren, "Robert Frost," *Yale Review,* XLIII (December 1953), 204–217.

Bowra, C. M., "Reassessments: Robert Frost," *Adelphi,* XXVII (November 1950), 46–64.

Breit, Harvey, "Talk with Robert Frost," *New York Times Book Review* (November 27, 1949), p. 20.

Brooks, Cleanth, *Modern Poetry and the Tradition,* Chapel Hill, N. C.: University of North Carolina, 1939.

——— and Robert Penn Warren, *Understanding Poetry,* rev. ed., New York: Holt, 1951.

Brower, Reuben A., "Something for Robert Frost," *New England Quarterly,* XXXIV (June 1961), 243–252.

Carlson, Eric W., "Robert Frost on 'Vocal Imagination, the Merger of Form and Content,'" *American Literature,* XXXIII (January 1962), 519–522.

Chatman, Seymour, "Robert Frost's 'Mowing': An Inquiry into Prosodic Structure," *Kenyon Review,* XVIII (Summer 1956), 421–438.

Ciardi, John, "Robert Frost, Master Conversationalist at Work," *Saturday Review,* XLII (March 21, 1959), 17–20.

——, "Robert Frost: The Way to the Poem," *Saturday Review,* XL (April 12, 1958), 13–15, 65.

Coffin, Robert P. Tristram, untitled review of *Fire and Ice, American Literature,* XIV (January 1943), 435–440.

Cook, Reginald L., "Notes on Frost the Lecturer," *Quarterly Journal of Speech,* XLII (April 1956), 127–132.

——, "Poet in the Mountains," *Western Review,* XI (Spring 1947), 175–181.

Coursen, Robert R., "A Dramatic Necessity: The Poetry of Robert Frost," *Bucknell Review,* X (December 1961), 138–147.

Cowley, Malcolm, "Frost: A Dissenting Opinion," *New Republic,* CLI (September 11, 1944), 312–313.

——, "The Case Against Mr. Frost," *New Republic,* CLI (September 18, 1944), 345–347.

Cox, James M., "Robert Frost and the Edge of the Clearing," *Virginia Quarterly Review,* XXXV (Winter 1959), 73–88.

Cox, Sidney, "The Sincerity of Robert Frost," *New Republic,* XII (August 25, 1917), 109–111.

Dabbs, J. McBride, "Robert Frost and the Dark Woods," *Yale Review,* XXIII (Spring 1934), 514–520.

Deen, Rosemary F., "The Voices of Robert Frost," *Commonweal,* LXIX (February 20, 1959), 542–544.

de Voto, Bernard, "The Critics and Robert Frost," *Saturday Review of Literature,* XVII (January 1, 1938), 3–4, 14–15.

Donoghue, Denis, "The Limitations of Robert Frost," *Twentieth Century*, CLXVI (July 1959), 13–22.

Frost, Robert, "The Art of Poetry II," *Paris Review*, No. XXIV (Summer-Fall 1960), 89–120.

———, "Education by Poetry: A Meditative Monologue," *Amherst Alumni Council News*, IV (March 1931), Supplement, 6–13.

———, Introduction to Edwin Arlington Robinson, *King Jasper*, New York: Macmillan, 1935.

———, "Maturity No Object," Introduction to *New Poets of England and America*, ed. Donald Hall et al., New York: Meridian, 1957.

———, "On Emerson," *Daedalus*, LXXXVIII (Fall 1959), 712–718.

———, "A Poet, Too, Must Learn the Magic Way of Poetry," *New York Times Book Review* (March 21, 1954), p. 1.

———, "Poetry and School," *Atlantic Monthly*, CLXXXVII (June 1951), 30–31.

———, Reginald Cook, and J. Isaacs, "Thoreau's Walden," *Listener*, LII (August 26, 1954), 319–320.

Garnett, Edward, "A New American Poet," *Atlantic Monthly*, CXVI (August 1915), 214–221.

Greenberg, Robert A., "Frost in England: A Publishing Incident," *New England Quarterly*, XXXIV (September 1961), 375–379.

Hepburn, James G., "Robert Frost and His Critics," *New England Quarterly*, XXXV (September 1962), 367–376.

Holmes, John, "Close-up of an American Poet at 75," *New York Times Magazine* (March 26, 1950), 12, 72–73, 75–77.

Hopkins, Vivian C., "Robert Frost: Out Far and In Deep," *Western Humanities Review*, XIV (Summer 1960), 247–263.

Irwin, W. R., "The Unity of Frost's Masques," *American Literature*, XXXII (November 1960), 302–312.

Jarrell, Randall, *Poetry and the Age*, New York: Knopf, 1955.

———, "Robert Frost's 'Home Burial,' " *The Moment of Poetry*, ed. Don Cameron Allen, Baltimore: Johns Hopkins University, 1962.

Langbaum, Robert, "The New Nature Poetry," *American Scholar*, XXVIII (Summer 1959), 323–340.

Lowell, Amy, *Tendencies in Modern American Poetry*, New York, Macmillan, 1917.

McLaughlin, Charles A., "Two Views of Poetic Unity," *University of Kansas City Review*, XXII (Summer 1956), 309–316.

Monroe, Harriet, *Poets and Their Art*, New York: Macmillan, 1926.

Montgomery, Marion, "Robert Frost and His Use of Barriers: Man vs. Nature towards God," *South Atlantic Quarterly*, LVII (Summer 1958), 339–353.

Mulder, William, "Freedom and Form: Robert Frost's Double Discipline," *South Atlantic Quarterly*, LIV (July 1955), 386–393.

Munford, Howard, "Frost's 'The Subverted Flower,' " *Explicator*, XVII (January 1959), item 31.

Napier, John T., "A Momentary Stay Against Confusion," *Virginia Quarterly Review*, XXXIII (Summer 1957), 378–394.

Newdick, Robert S., "Robert Frost and the Dramatic," *New England Quarterly*, X (June 1937), 262–269.

———, "Robert Frost and the Sound of Sense," *American Literature*, IX (November 1937), 289–300.

O'Donnell, William G., "Robert Frost and New England," *Yale Review*, XXXVII (Summer 1948), 698–712.

Ogilvie, John T., "From Woods to Stars: A Pattern of Imagery in Robert Frost's Poetry," *South Atlantic Quarterly,* LVIII (Winter 1959), 64–76.

Pearce, Roy Harvey, "Frost's Momentary Stay," *Kenyon Review,* XXIII (Spring 1961), 258–273.

Perrine, Laurence, *Sound and Sense,* New York: Harcourt, 1956.

Pound, Ezra, *Literary Essays,* New York: New Directions, 1954.

Pritchard, William H., "Diminished Nature," *Massachusetts Review,* I (May 1960), 475–492.

———, "*North of Boston:* Frost's Poetry of Dialogue," *In Defense of Reading,* ed. Reuben A. Brower and Richard Poirer, New York: Dutton, 1962.

Rukeyser, Muriel, "In a Speaking Voice," *Poetry,* LIV (July 1939), 218–224.

Ryan, Alvan S., "Frost and Emerson: Voice and Vision," *Massachusetts Review,* I (October 1959), 5–23.

Scott, Winfield Townley, "Frost's Seventh Book," *Poetry,* LX (June 1942), 146–149.

Simpson, Claude M., "Robert Frost and Man's 'Royal Role,' " *Aspects of American Poetry,* ed. Richard M. Ludwig, Columbus: Ohio State University, 1962.

Stallman, R. W., "The Position of Poetry Today," *English Journal,* XLVI (May 1957), 241–251.

Stauffer, Donald B., "Frost's 'The Subverted Flower,' " *Explicator,* XV (March 1957), item 38.

Thompson, Lawrance, "A Native to the Grain of the American Idiom," *Saturday Review,* XLII (March 21, 1959), 21, 55–56.

Thorp, Willard, "The New Poetry," *Literary History of the United States,* ed. Robert E. Spiller et al., New York: Macmillan, 1949, II, 1189–1196.

Trilling, Lionel, "A Speech on Robert Frost: A Cultural Episode," *Partisan Review*, XXVI (Summer 1959), 445–452.

Untermeyer, Louis, *From Another World*, New York: Harcourt, 1939.

——, "Our Singing Faith," *Saturday Review of Literature*, VII (January 17, 1931), 529–530.

——, *The Road Not Taken*, New York: Holt, 1951.

Van Doren, Mark, "The Permanence of Robert Frost," *American Scholar*, V (Spring 1936), 190–198.

——, "Robert Frost's America," *Atlantic Monthly*, CLXXXVII (June 1951), 32–34.

Waggoner, Hyatt Howe, *The Heel of Elohim*, Norman: University of Oklahoma, 1950.

——, "The Humanistic Idealism of Robert Frost," *American Literature*, XIII (November 1941), 207–223.

Walcutt, Charles Child, "Interpreting the Symbol," *College English*, XIV (May 1953), 446–454.

Warren, Robert Penn, *Selected Essays*, New York: Random House, 1958.

Watts, Harold H., "Robert Frost and the Interrupted Dialogue," *American Literature*, XXVII (March 1955), 69–87.

Wells, Henry W., *The American Way of Poetry*, New York: Columbia University, 1943.

Whicher, George F., "Frost at Seventy," *American Scholar*, XIV (Autumn 1945), 405–414.

——, "Out for Stars," *Atlantic Monthly*, CLXXI (May 1943), 64–67.

Whipple, T. K., *Spokesmen*, New York: Appleton, 1928.

Willige, Eckhart, "Formal Devices in Robert Frost's Short Poems," *Georgia Review*, XV (Fall 1961), 324–330.

Winters, Yvor, *The Function of Criticism*, Denver: Alan Swallow, 1957.

The Figure a Poem Makes

ABSTRACTION is an old story with the philosophers, but it has been like a new toy in the hands of the artists of our day. Why can't we have any one quality of poetry we choose by itself? We can have in thought. Then it will go hard if we can't in practice. Our lives for it.

Granted no one but a humanist much cares how sound a poem is if it is only *a* sound. The sound is the gold in the ore. Then we will have the sound out alone and dispense with the inessential. We do till we make the discovery that the object in writing poetry is to make all poems sound as different as possible from each other, and the resources for that of vowels, consonants, punctuation, syntax, words, sentences, meter are not enough. We need the help of context—meaning—subject matter. That is the greatest help towards variety. All that can be done with words is soon told. So also with meters—particularly in our language where there are virtually but two, strict iambic and loose iambic. The ancients with many were still poor if they depended on meters for all tune. It is painful to watch our sprung-rhythmists straining at the point of omitting one short from a foot for relief from monotony. The possibilities for tune from the dramatic tones of meaning struck across the rigidity of a limited meter are endless. And we are back in poetry as merely one more art of having something to say, sound or unsound. Probably better if sound, because deeper and from wider experience.

Then there is this wildness whereof it is spoken. Granted again that it has an equal claim with sound to being a poem's better half. If it is a wild tune, it is a poem. Our problem then is, as modern abstractionists, to have the wildness pure; to be wild with nothing to be wild about. We bring up as aberrationists, giving way to undirected associations and kicking ourselves from one chance suggestion to another in all directions as of a hot afternoon in the life of a grasshopper. Theme alone can steady us down. Just as the first mystery was how a poem could have a tune in such a straightness as meter, so the second mystery is how a poem can have wildness and at the same time a subject that shall be fulfilled.

It should be of the pleasure of a poem itself to tell how it can. The figure a poem makes. It begins in delight and ends in wisdom. The figure is the same as for love. No one can really hold that the ecstasy should be static and stand still in one place. It begins in delight, it inclines to the impulse, it assumes direction with the first line laid down, it runs a course of lucky events, and ends in a clarification of life—not necessarily a great clarification, such as sects and cults are founded on, but in a momentary stay against confusion. It has denouement. It has an outcome that though unforeseen was predestined from the first image of the original mood—and indeed from the very mood. It is but a trick poem and no poem at all if the best of it was thought of first and saved for the last. It finds its own name as it goes and discovers the best waiting for it in some final phrase at once wise and sad—the happy-sad blend of the drinking song.

No tears in the writer, no tears in the reader. No surprise

for the writer, no surprise for the reader. For me the initial delight is in the surprise of remembering something I didn't know I knew. I am in a place, in a situation, as if I had materialized from cloud or risen out of the ground. There is a glad recognition of the long lost and the rest follows. Step by step the wonder of unexpected supply keeps growing. The impressions most useful to my purpose seem always those I was unaware of and so made no note of at the time when taken, and the conclusion is come to that like giants we are always hurling experience ahead of us to pave the future with against the day when we may want to strike a line of purpose across it for somewhere. The line will have the more charm for not being mechanically straight. We enjoy the straight crookedness of a good walking stick. Modern instruments of precision are being used to make things crooked as if by eye and hand in the old days.

I tell how there may be a better wildness of logic than of inconsequence. But the logic is backward, in retrospect, after the act. It must be more felt than seen ahead like prophecy. It must be a revelation, or a series of revelations, as much for the poet as for the reader. For it to be that there must have been the greatest freedom of the material to move about in it and to establish relations in it regardless of time and space, previous relation, and everything but affinity. We prate of freedom. We call our schools free because we are not free to stay away from them till we are sixteen years of age. I have given up my democratic prejudices and now willingly set the lower classes free to be completely taken care of by the upper classes. Political freedom is nothing to me. I bestow it right and left. All I would keep for myself is the freedom of my material—the condition of body and mind now and then to summons aptly from the vast chaos of all I have lived through.

Scholars and artists thrown together are often annoyed at the puzzle of where they differ. Both work from knowledge;

3

but I suspect they differ most importantly in the way their knowledge is come by. Scholars get theirs with conscientious thoroughness along projected lines of logic; poets theirs cavalierly and as it happens in and out of books. They stick to nothing deliberately, but let what will stick to them like burrs where they walk in the fields. No acquirement is on assignment, or even self-assignment. Knowledge of the second kind is much more available in the wild free ways of wit and art. A schoolboy may be defined as one who can tell you what he knows in the order in which he learned it. The artist must value himself as he snatches a thing from some previous order in time and space into a new order with not so much as a ligature clinging to it of the old place where it was organic.

More than once I should have lost my soul to radicalism if it had been the originality it was mistaken for by its young converts. Originality and initiative are what I ask for my country. For myself the originality need be no more than the freshness of a poem run in the way I have described: from delight to wisdom. The figure is the same as for love. Like a piece of ice on a hot stove the poem must ride on its own melting. A poem may be worked over once it is in being, but may not be worried into being. Its most precious quality will remain its having run itself and carried away the poet with it. Read it a hundred times: it will forever keep its freshness as a metal keeps its fragrance. It can never lose its sense of a meaning that once unfolded by surprise as it went.

R. F.

A Boy's Will

THE PASTURE

I'm going out to clean the pasture spring;
I'll only stop to rake the leaves away
(And wait to watch the water clear, I may):
I sha'n't be gone long.—You come too.

I'm going out to fetch the little calf
That's standing by the mother. It's so young
It totters when she licks it with her tongue.
I sha'n't be gone long.—You come too.

INTO MY OWN

One of my wishes is that those dark trees,
So old and firm they scarcely show the breeze,
Were not, as 'twere, the merest mask of gloom,
But stretched away unto the edge of doom.

5

I should not be withheld but that some day
Into their vastness I should steal away,
Fearless of ever finding open land,
Or highway where the slow wheel pours the sand.

I do not see why I should e'er turn back,
Or those should not set forth upon my track
To overtake me, who should miss me here
And long to know if still I held them dear.

They would not find me changed from him they knew—
Only more sure of all I thought was true.

GHOST HOUSE

I dwell in a lonely house I know
That vanished many a summer ago,
    And left no trace but the cellar walls,
    And a cellar in which the daylight falls,
And the purple-stemmed wild raspberries grow.

O'er ruined fences the grapevines shield
The woods come back to the mowing field;
    The orchard tree has grown one copse
    Of new wood and old where the woodpecker chops;
The footpath down to the well is healed.

I dwell with a strangely aching heart
In that vanished abode there far apart
    On that disused and forgotten road
    That has no dust-bath now for the toad.
Night comes; the black bats tumble and dart;

The whippoorwill is coming to shout
And hush and cluck and flutter about:
   I hear him begin far enough away
   Full many a time to say his say
Before he arrives to say it out.

It is under the small, dim, summer star.
I know not who these mute folk are
   Who share the unlit place with me—
   Those stones out under the low-limbed tree
Doubtless bear names that the mosses mar.

They are tireless folk, but slow and sad,
Though two, close-keeping, are lass and lad,—
   With none among them that ever sings,
   And yet, in view of how many things,
As sweet companions as might be had.

MY NOVEMBER GUEST

My Sorrow, when she's here with me,
   Thinks these dark days of autumn rain
Are beautiful as days can be;
She loves the bare, the withered tree;
   She walks the sodden pasture lane.

Her pleasure will not let me stay.
   She talks and I am fain to list:
She's glad the birds are gone away,
She's glad her simple worsted gray
   Is silver now with clinging mist.

7

The desolate, deserted trees,
    The faded earth, the heavy sky,
The beauties she so truly sees,
She thinks I have no eye for these,
    And vexes me for reason why.

Not yesterday I learned to know
    The love of bare November days
Before the coming of the snow,
But it were vain to tell her so.
    And they are better for her praise.

LOVE AND A QUESTION

A Stranger came to the door at eve,
    And he spoke the bridegroom fair.
He bore a green-white stick in his hand,
    And, for all burden, care.
He asked with the eyes more than the lips
    For a shelter for the night,
And he turned and looked at the road afar
    Without a window light.

The bridegroom came forth into the porch
    With 'Let us look at the sky,
And question what of the night to be,
    Stranger, you and I.'
The woodbine leaves littered the yard,
    The woodbine berries were blue,
Autumn, yes, winter was in the wind;
    'Stranger, I wish I knew.'

A Late Walk

Within, the bride in the dusk alone
    Bent over the open fire,
Her face rose-red with the glowing coal
    And the thought of the heart's desire.
The bridegroom looked at the weary road,
    Yet saw but her within,
And wished her heart in a case of gold
    And pinned with a silver pin.

The bridegroom thought it little to give
    A dole of bread, a purse,
A heartfelt prayer for the poor of God,
    Or for the rich a curse;
But whether or not a man was asked
    To mar the love of two
By harboring woe in the bridal house,
    The bridegroom wished he knew.

A LATE WALK

When I go up through the mowing field,
    The headless aftermath,
Smooth-laid like thatch with the heavy dew,
    Half closes the garden path.

And when I come to the garden ground,
    The whir of sober birds
Up from the tangle of withered weeds
    Is sadder than any words.

A tree beside the wall stands bare,
    But a leaf that lingered brown,
Disturbed, I doubt not, by my thought,
    Comes softly rattling down.

I end not far from my going forth
    By picking the faded blue
Of the last remaining aster flower
    To carry again to you.

STORM FEAR

When the wind works against us in the dark,
And pelts with snow
The lower chamber window on the east,
And whispers with a sort of stifled bark,
The beast,
'Come out! Come out!'—
It costs no inward struggle not to go,
Ah, no!
I count our strength,
Two and a child,
Those of us not asleep subdued to mark
How the cold creeps as the fire dies at length,—
How drifts are piled,
Dooryard and road ungraded,
Till even the comforting barn grows far away,
And my heart owns a doubt
Whether 'tis in us to arise with day
And save ourselves unaided.

TO THE THAWING WIND

Come with rain, O loud Southwester!
Bring the singer, bring the nester;
Give the buried flower a dream;
Make the settled snowbank steam;
Find the brown beneath the white;
But whate'er you do tonight,
Bathe my window, make it flow,
Melt it as the ice will go;
Melt the glass and leave the sticks
Like a hermit's crucifix;
Burst into my narrow stall;
Swing the picture on the wall;
Run the rattling pages o'er;
Scatter poems on the floor;
Turn the poet out of door.

A PRAYER IN SPRING

Oh, give us pleasure in the flowers today;
And give us not to think so far away
As the uncertain harvest; keep us here
All simply in the springing of the year.

Oh, give us pleasure in the orchard white,
Like nothing else by day, like ghosts by night;
And make us happy in the happy bees,
The swarm dilating round the perfect trees.

And make us happy in the darting bird
That suddenly above the bees is heard,
The meteor that thrusts in with needle bill,
And off a blossom in mid air stands still.

For this is love and nothing else is love,
The which it is reserved for God above
To sanctify to what far ends He will,
But which it only needs that we fulfill.

ROSE POGONIAS

A saturated meadow,
   Sun-shaped and jewel-small,
A circle scarcely wider
   Than the trees around were tall;
Where winds were quite excluded,
   And the air was stifling sweet
With the breath of many flowers,—
   A temple of the heat.

There we bowed us in the burning,
   As the sun's right worship is,
To pick where none could miss them
   A thousand orchises;
For though the grass was scattered,
   Yet every second spear
Seemed tipped with wings of color,
   That tinged the atmosphere.

We raised a simple prayer
   Before we left the spot,

That in the general mowing
    That place might be forgot;
Or if not all so favored,
    Obtain such grace of hours,
That none should mow the grass there
    While so confused with flowers.

WAITING

AFIELD AT DUSK

What things for dream there are when specter-like,
Moving along tall haycocks lightly piled,
I enter alone upon the stubble field,
From which the laborers' voices late have died,
And in the antiphony of afterglow
And rising full moon, sit me down
Upon the full moon's side of the first haycock
And lose myself amid so many alike.

I dream upon the opposing lights of the hour,
Preventing shadow until the moon prevail;
I dream upon the nighthawks peopling heaven,
Each circling each with vague unearthly cry,
Or plunging headlong with fierce twang afar;
And on the bat's mute antics, who would seem
Dimly to have made out my secret place,
Only to lose it when he pirouettes,
And seek it endlessly with purblind haste;
On the last swallow's sweep; and on the rasp
In the abyss of odor and rustle at my back,
That, silenced by my advent, finds once more,
After an interval, his instrument,

13

And tries once—twice—and thrice if I be there;
And on the worn book of old-golden song
I brought not here to read, it seems, but hold
And freshen in this air of withering sweetness;
But on the memory of one absent most,
For whom these lines when they shall greet her eye.

IN NEGLECT

They leave us so to the way we took,
    As two in whom they were proved mistaken,
That we sit sometimes in the wayside nook,
With mischievous, vagrant, seraphic look,
    And *try* if we cannot feel forsaken.

THE VANTAGE POINT

If tired of trees I seek again mankind,
    Well I know where to hie me—in the dawn,
    To a slope where the cattle keep the lawn.
There amid lolling juniper reclined,
Myself unseen, I see in white defined
    Far off the homes of men, and farther still,
    The graves of men on an opposing hill,
Living or dead, whichever are to mind.

And if by noon I have too much of these,
    I have but to turn on my arm, and lo,
    The sun-burned hillside sets my face aglow,
My breathing shakes the bluet like a breeze,
    I smell the earth, I smell the bruisèd plant,
    I look into the crater of the ant.

MOWING

There was never a sound beside the wood but one,
And that was my long scythe whispering to the ground.
What was it it whispered? I knew not well myself;
Perhaps it was something about the heat of the sun,
Something, perhaps, about the lack of sound—
And that was why it whispered and did not speak.
It was no dream of the gift of idle hours,
Or easy gold at the hand of fay or elf:
Anything more than the truth would have seemed too weak
To the earnest love that laid the swale in rows,
Not without feeble-pointed spikes of flowers
(Pale orchises), and scared a bright green snake.
The fact is the sweetest dream that labor knows.
My long scythe whispered and left the hay to make.

REVELATION

We make ourselves a place apart
 Behind light words that tease and flout,
But oh, the agitated heart
 Till someone really find us out.

'Tis pity if the case require
 (Or so we say) that in the end
We speak the literal to inspire
 The understanding of a friend.

But so with all, from babes that play
 At hide-and-seek to God afar,
So all who hide too well away
 Must speak and tell us where they are.

THE TRIAL BY EXISTENCE

Even the bravest that are slain
    Shall not dissemble their surprise
On waking to find valor reign,
    Even as on earth, in paradise;
And where they sought without the sword
    Wide fields of asphodel fore'er,
To find that the utmost reward
    Of daring should be still to dare.

The light of heaven falls whole and white
    And is not shattered into dyes,
The light forever is morning light;
    The hills are verdured pasture-wise;
The angel hosts with freshness go,
    And seek with laughter what to brave;—
And binding all is the hushed snow
    Of the far-distant breaking wave.

And from a cliff-top is proclaimed
    The gathering of the souls for birth,
The trial by existence named,
    The obscuration upon earth.
And the slant spirits trooping by
    In streams and cross- and counter-streams
Can but give ear to that sweet cry
    For its suggestion of what dreams!

And the more loitering are turned
    To view once more the sacrifice
Of those who for some good discerned
    Will gladly give up paradise.

And a white shimmering concourse rolls
   Toward the throne to witness there
The speeding of devoted souls
   Which God makes his especial care.

And none are taken but who will,
   Having first heard the life read out
That opens earthward, good and ill,
   Beyond the shadow of a doubt;
And very beautifully God limns,
   And tenderly, life's little dream,
But naught extenuates or dims,
   Setting the thing that is supreme.

Nor is there wanting in the press
   Some spirit to stand simply forth,
Heroic in its nakedness,
   Against the uttermost of earth.
The tale of earth's unhonored things
   Sounds nobler there than 'neath the sun;
And the mind whirls and the heart sings,
   And a shout greets the daring one.

But always God speaks at the end:
   'One thought in agony of strife
The bravest would have by for friend,
   The memory that he chose the life;
But the pure fate to which you go
   Admits no memory of choice,
Or the woe were not earthly woe
   To which you give the assenting voice.'

And so the choice must be again,
   But the last choice is still the same;

And the awe passes wonder then,
   And a hush falls for all acclaim.
And God has taken a flower of gold
   And broken it, and used therefrom
The mystic link to bind and hold
   Spirit to matter till death come.

'Tis of the essence of life here,
   Though we choose greatly, still to lack
The lasting memory at all clear,
   That life has for us on the wrack
Nothing but what we somehow chose;
   Thus are we wholly stripped of pride
In the pain that has but one close,
   Bearing it crushed and mystified.

THE TUFT OF FLOWERS

I went to turn the grass once after one
Who mowed it in the dew before the sun.

The dew was gone that made his blade so keen
Before I came to view the leveled scene.

I looked for him behind an isle of trees;
I listened for his whetstone on the breeze.

But he had gone his way, the grass all mown,
And I must be, as he had been,—alone,

'As all must be,' I said within my heart,
'Whether they work together or apart.'

But as I said it, swift there passed me by
On noiseless wing a bewildered butterfly,

Seeking with memories grown dim o'er night
Some resting flower of yesterday's delight.

And once I marked his flight go round and round,
As where some flower lay withering on the ground.

And then he flew as far as eye could see,
And then on tremulous wing came back to me.

I thought of questions that have no reply,
And would have turned to toss the grass to dry;

But he turned first, and led my eye to look
At a tall tuft of flowers beside a brook,

A leaping tongue of bloom the scythe had spared
Beside a reedy brook the scythe had bared.

The mower in the dew had loved them thus,
By leaving them to flourish, not for us,

Nor yet to draw one thought of ours to him,
But from sheer morning gladness at the brim.

The butterfly and I had lit upon,
Nevertheless, a message from the dawn,

That made me hear the wakening birds around,
And hear his long scythe whispering to the ground,

And feel a spirit kindred to my own;
So that henceforth I worked no more alone;

But glad with him, I worked as with his aid,
And weary, sought at noon with him the shade;

And dreaming, as it were, held brotherly speech
With one whose thought I had not hoped to reach.

'Men work together,' I told him from the heart,
'Whether they work together or apart.'

THE DEMIURGE'S LAUGH

It was far in the sameness of the wood;
   I was running with joy on the Demon's trail,
Though I knew what I hunted was no true god.
   It was just as the light was beginning to fail
That I suddenly heard—all I needed to hear:
It has lasted me many and many a year.

The sound was behind me instead of before,
   A sleepy sound, but mocking half,
As of one who utterly couldn't care.
   The Demon arose from his wallow to laugh,
Brushing the dirt from his eye as he went;
And well I knew what the Demon meant.

I shall not forget how his laugh rang out.
   I felt as a fool to have been so caught,
And checked my steps to make pretense
   It was something among the leaves I sought
(Though doubtful whether he stayed to see).
Thereafter I sat me against a tree.

OCTOBER

O hushed October morning mild,
Thy leaves have ripened to the fall;
Tomorrow's wind, if it be wild,
Should waste them all.
The crows above the forest call;
Tomorrow they may form and go.
O hushed October morning mild,
Begin the hours of this day slow.
Make the day seem to us less brief.
Hearts not averse to being beguiled,
Beguile us in the way you know.
Release one leaf at break of day;
At noon release another leaf;
One from our trees, one far away.
Retard the sun with gentle mist;
Enchant the land with amethyst.
Slow, slow!
For the grapes' sake, if they were all,
Whose leaves already are burnt with frost,
Whose clustered fruit must else be lost—
For the grapes' sake along the wall.

RELUCTANCE

Out through the fields and the woods
   And over the walls I have wended;
I have climbed the hills of view
   And looked at the world, and descended;
I have come by the highway home,
   And lo, it is ended.

The leaves are all dead on the ground,
    Save those that the oak is keeping
To ravel them one by one
    And let them go scraping and creeping
Out over the crusted snow,
    When others are sleeping.

And the dead leaves lie huddled and still
    No longer blown hither and thither;
The last lone aster is gone;
    The flowers of the witch-hazel wither,
The heart is still aching to seek,
    But the feet question 'Whither?'

Ah, when to the heart of man
    Was it ever less than a treason
To go with the drift of things,
    To yield with a grace to reason,
And bow and accept the end
    Of a love or a season?

North of Boston

MENDING WALL

Something there is that doesn't love a wall,
That sends the frozen-ground-swell under it,
And spills the upper boulders in the sun;
And makes gaps even two can pass abreast.
The work of hunters is another thing:
I have come after them and made repair
Where they have left not one stone on a stone,
But they would have the rabbit out of hiding,
To please the yelping dogs. The gaps I mean,
No one has seen them made or heard them made,
But at spring mending-time we find them there.
I let my neighbor know beyond the hill;
And on a day we meet to walk the line
And set the wall between us once again.
We keep the wall between us as we go.
To each the boulders that have fallen to each.
And some are loaves and some so nearly balls
We have to use a spell to make them balance:

'Stay where you are until our backs are turned!'
We wear our fingers rough with handling them.
Oh, just another kind of outdoor game,
One on a side. It comes to little more:
There where it is we do not need the wall:
He is all pine and I am apple orchard.
My apple trees will never get across
And eat the cones under his pines, I tell him.
He only says, 'Good fences make good neighbors.'
Spring is the mischief in me, and I wonder
If I could put a notion in his head:
'*Why* do they make good neighbors? Isn't it
Where there are cows? But here there are no cows.
Before I built a wall I'd ask to know
What I was walling in or walling out,
And to whom I was like to give offense.
Something there is that doesn't love a wall,
That wants it down.' I could say 'Elves' to him,
But it's not elves exactly, and I'd rather
He said it for himself. I see him there
Bringing a stone grasped firmly by the top
In each hand, like an old-stone savage armed.
He moves in darkness as it seems to me,
Not of woods only and the shade of trees.
He will not go behind his father's saying,
And he likes having thought of it so well
He says again, 'Good fences make good neighbors.'

THE DEATH OF THE HIRED MAN

Mary sat musing on the lamp-flame at the table
Waiting for Warren. When she heard his step,
She ran on tip-toe down the darkened passage
To meet him in the doorway with the news
And put him on his guard. 'Silas is back.'
She pushed him outward with her through the door
And shut it after her. 'Be kind,' she said.
She took the market things from Warren's arms
And set them on the porch, then drew him down
To sit beside her on the wooden steps.

'When was I ever anything but kind to him?
But I'll not have the fellow back,' he said.
'I told him so last haying, didn't I?
If he left then, I said, that ended it.
What good is he? Who else will harbor him
At his age for the little he can do?
What help he is there's no depending on.
Off he goes always when I need him most.
He thinks he ought to earn a little pay,
Enough at least to buy tobacco with,
So he won't have to beg and be beholden.
"All right," I say, "I can't afford to pay
Any fixed wages, though I wish I could."
"Someone else can." "Then someone else will have to."
I shouldn't mind his bettering himself
If that was what it was. You can be certain,
When he begins like that, there's someone at him
Trying to coax him off with pocket-money,—
In haying time, when any help is scarce.
In winter he comes back to us. I'm done.'

'Sh! not so loud: he'll hear you,' Mary said.

'I want him to: he'll have to soon or late.'

'He's worn out. He's asleep beside the stove.
When I came up from Rowe's I found him here,
Huddled against the barn-door fast asleep,
A miserable sight, and frightening, too—
You needn't smile—I didn't recognize him—
I wasn't looking for him—and he's changed.
Wait till you see.'

     'Where did you say he'd been?'

'He didn't say. I dragged him to the house,
And gave him tea and tried to make him smoke.
I tried to make him talk about his travels.
Nothing would do: he just kept nodding off.'

'What did he say? Did he say anything?'

'But little.'

   'Anything? Mary, confess
He said he'd come to ditch the meadow for me.'

'Warren!'

    'But did he? I just want to know.'

'Of course he did. What would you have him say?
Surely you wouldn't grudge the poor old man
Some humble way to save his self-respect.
He added, if you really care to know,
He meant to clear the upper pasture, too.
That sounds like something you have heard before?
Warren, I wish you could have heard the way
He jumbled everything. I stopped to look
Two or three times—he made me feel so queer—
To see if he was talking in his sleep.

He ran on Harold Wilson—you remember—
The boy you had in haying four years since.
He's finished school, and teaching in his college.
Silas declares you'll have to get him back.
He says they two will make a team for work:
Between them they will lay this farm as smooth!
The way he mixed that in with other things.
He thinks young Wilson a likely lad, though daft
On education—you know how they fought
All through July under the blazing sun,
Silas up on the cart to build the load,
Harold along beside to pitch it on.'

'Yes, I took care to keep well out of earshot.'

'Well, those days trouble Silas like a dream.
You wouldn't think they would. How some things linger!
Harold's young college boy's assurance piqued him.
After so many years he still keeps finding
Good arguments he sees he might have used.
I sympathize. I know just how it feels
To think of the right thing to say too late.
Harold's associated in his mind with Latin.
He asked me what I thought of Harold's saying
He studied Latin like the violin
Because he liked it—that an argument!
He said he couldn't make the boy believe
He could find water with a hazel prong—
Which showed how much good school had ever done him.
He wanted to go over that. But most of all
He thinks if he could have another chance
To teach him how to build a load of hay—'

'I know, that's Silas' one accomplishment.
He bundles every forkful in its place,

And tags and numbers it for future reference,
So he can find and easily dislodge it
In the unloading. Silas does that well.
He takes it out in bunches like big birds' nests.
You never see him standing on the hay
He's trying to lift, straining to lift himself.'

'He thinks if he could teach him that, he'd be
Some good perhaps to someone in the world.
He hates to see a boy the fool of books.
Poor Silas, so concerned for other folk,
And nothing to look backward to with pride,
And nothing to look forward to with hope,
So now and never any different.'

Part of a moon was falling down the west,
Dragging the whole sky with it to the hills.
Its light poured softly in her lap. She saw it
And spread her apron to it. She put out her hand
Among the harp-like morning-glory strings,
Taut with the dew from garden bed to eaves,
As if she played unheard some tenderness
That wrought on him beside her in the night.
'Warren,' she said, 'he has come home to die:
You needn't be afraid he'll leave you this time.'

'Home,' he mocked gently.

                     'Yes, what else but home?
It all depends on what you mean by home.
Of course he's nothing to us, any more
Than was the hound that came a stranger to us
Out of the woods, worn out upon the trail.'

'Home is the place where, when you have to go there,
They have to take you in.'

The Death of the Hired Man

       'I should have called **it**
Something you somehow haven't to deserve.'

Warren leaned out and took a step or two,
Picked up a little stick, and brought it back
And broke it in his hand and tossed it by.
'Silas has better claim on us you think
Than on his brother? Thirteen little miles
As the road winds would bring him to his door.
Silas has walked that far no doubt today.
Why doesn't he go there? His brother's rich,
A somebody—director in the bank.'

'He never told us that.'

       'We know it though.'

'I think his brother ought to help, of course.
I'll see to that if there is need. He ought of right
To take him in, and might be willing to—
He may be better than appearances.
But have some pity on Silas. Do you think
If he had any pride in claiming kin
Or anything he looked for from his brother,
He'd keep so still about him all this time?'

'I wonder what's between them.'

        'I can tell you.
Silas is what he is—we wouldn't mind him—
But just the kind that kinsfolk can't abide.
He never did a thing so very bad.
He don't know why he isn't quite as good
As anybody. Worthless though he is,
He won't be made ashamed to please his brother.'

'*I* can't think Si ever hurt anyone.'

'No, but he hurt my heart the way he lay
And rolled his old head on that sharp-edged chair-back.
He wouldn't let me put him on the lounge.
You must go in and see what you can do.
I made the bed up for him there tonight.
You'll be surprised at him—how much he's broken.
His working days are done; I'm sure of it.'

'I'd not be in a hurry to say that.'

'I haven't been. Go, look, see for yourself.
But, Warren, please remember how it is:
He's come to help you ditch the meadow.
He has a plan. You mustn't laugh at him.
He may not speak of it, and then he may.
I'll sit and see if that small sailing cloud
Will hit or miss the moon.'

　　　　　　　　　It hit the moon.
Then there were three there, making a dim row,
The moon, the little silver cloud, and she.

Warren returned—too soon, it seemed to her,
Slipped to her side, caught up her hand and waited.

'Warren?' she questioned.

　　　　　　　　'Dead,' was all he answered.

THE MOUNTAIN

The mountain held the town as in a shadow.
I saw so much before I slept there once:
I noticed that I missed stars in the west,
Where its black body cut into the sky.
Near me it seemed: I felt it like a wall
Behind which I was sheltered from a wind.
And yet between the town and it I found,
When I walked forth at dawn to see new things,
Were fields, a river, and beyond, more fields.
The river at the time was fallen away,
And made a widespread brawl on cobblestones;
But the signs showed what it had done in spring:
Good grassland gullied out, and in the grass
Ridges of sand, and driftwood stripped of bark.
I crossed the river and swung round the mountain.
And there I met a man who moved so slow
With white-faced oxen in a heavy cart,
It seemed no harm to stop him altogether.

'What town is this?' I asked.

                'This? Lunenburg.'

Then I was wrong: the town of my sojourn,
Beyond the bridge, was not that of the mountain,
But only felt at night its shadowy presence.
'Where is your village? Very far from here?'

'There is no village—only scattered farms.
We were but sixty voters last election.
We can't in nature grow to many more:
That thing takes all the room!' He moved his goad.
The mountain stood there to be pointed at.
Pasture ran up the side a little way,

And then there was a wall of trees with trunks;
After that only tops of trees, and cliffs
Imperfectly concealed among the leaves.
A dry ravine emerged from under boughs
Into the pasture.

        'That looks like a path.
Is that the way to reach the top from here?—
Not for this morning, but some other time:
I must be getting back to breakfast now.'

'I don't advise your trying from this side.
There is no proper path, but those that *have*
Been up, I understand, have climbed from Ladd's.
That's five miles back. You can't mistake the place:
They logged it there last winter some way up.
I'd take you, but I'm bound the other way.'

'You've never climbed it?'
             'I've been on the sides,
Deer-hunting and trout-fishing. There's a brook
That starts up on it somewhere—I've heard say
Right on the top, tip-top—a curious thing.
But what would interest you about the brook,
It's always cold in summer, warm in winter.
One of the great sights going is to see
It steam in winter like an ox's breath,
Until the bushes all along its banks
Are inch-deep with the frosty spines and bristles—
You know the kind. Then let the sun shine on it!'

'There ought to be a view around the world
From such a mountain—if it isn't wooded
Clear to the top.' I saw through leafy screens
Great granite terraces in sun and shadow,

Shelves one could rest a knee on getting up—
With depths behind him sheer a hundred feet.
Or turn and sit on and look out and down,
With little ferns in crevices at his elbow.

'As to that I can't say. But there's the spring,
Right on the summit, almost like a fountain.
That ought to be worth seeing.'

                            'If it's there.
You never saw it?'

                        'I guess there's no doubt
About its being there. I never saw it.
It may not be right on the very top:
It wouldn't have to be a long way down
To have some head of water from above,
And a *good distance* down might not be noticed
By anyone who'd come a long way up.
One time I asked a fellow climbing it
To look and tell me later how it was.'

'What did he say?'

                       'He said there was a lake
Somewhere in Ireland on a mountain top.'

'But a lake's different. What about the spring?'

'He never got up high enough to see.
That's why I don't advise your trying this side.
He tried this side. I've always meant to go
And look myself, but you know how it is:
It doesn't seem so much to climb a mountain
You've worked around the foot of all your life.
What would I do? Go in my overalls,
With a big stick, the same as when the cows

Haven't come down to the bars at milking time?
Or with a shotgun for a stray black bear?
'Twouldn't seem real to climb for climbing it.'

'I shouldn't climb it if I didn't want to—
Not for the sake of climbing. What's its name?'

'We call it Hor: I don't know if that's right.'

'Can one walk around it? Would it be too far?'

'You can drive round and keep in Lunenburg,
But it's as much as ever you can do,
The boundary lines keep in so close to it.
Hor is the township, and the township's Hor—
And a few houses sprinkled round the foot,
Like boulders broken off the upper cliff,
Rolled out a little farther than the rest.'

'Warm in December, cold in June, you say?'

'I don't suppose the water's changed at all.
You and I know enough to know it's warm
Compared with cold, and cold compared with warm
But all the fun's in how you say a thing.'

'You've lived here all your life?'

                          'Ever since Hor
Was no bigger than a—' What, I did not hear.
He drew the oxen toward him with light touches
Of his slim goad on nose and offside flank,
Gave them their marching orders and was moving.

A HUNDRED COLLARS

Lancaster bore him—such a little town,
Such a great man. It doesn't see him often
Of late years, though he keeps the old homestead
And sends the children down there with their mother
To run wild in the summer—a little wild.
Sometimes he joins them for a day or two
And sees old friends he somehow can't get near.
They meet him in the general store at night,
Preoccupied with formidable mail,
Rifling a printed letter as he talks.
They seem afraid. He wouldn't have it so:
Though a great scholar, he's a democrat,
If not at heart, at least on principle.
Lately when coming up to Lancaster,
His train being late, he missed another train
And had four hours to wait at Woodsville Junction
After eleven o'clock at night. Too tired
To think of sitting such an ordeal out,
He turned to the hotel to find a bed.

'No room,' the night clerk said. 'Unless—'

Woodsville's a place of shrieks and wandering lamps
And cars that shock and rattle—and *one* hotel.

'You say "unless." '

                    'Unless you wouldn't mind
Sharing a room with someone else.'

                              'Who is it?'

'A man.'

          'So I should hope. What kind of man?'

'I know him: he's all right. A man's a man.
Separate beds, of course, you understand.'
The night clerk blinked his eyes and dared him on.

'Who's that man sleeping in the office chair?
Has he had the refusal of my chance?'

'He was afraid of being robbed or murdered.
What do you say?'

     'I'll have to have a bed.'

The night clerk led him up three flights of stairs
And down a narrow passage full of doors,
At the last one of which he knocked and entered.
'Lafe, here's a fellow wants to share your room.'

'Show him this way. I'm not afraid of him.
I'm not so drunk I can't take care of myself.'

The night clerk clapped a bedstead on the foot.
'This will be yours. Good-night,' he said, and went.

'Lafe was the name, I think?'

       'Yes, *Lay*fayette.
You got it the first time. And yours?'

        'Magoon.
Doctor Magoon.'

    'A Doctor?'

       'Well, a teacher.'

'Professor Square-the-circle-till-you're-tired?
Hold on, there's something I don't think of now
That I had on my mind to ask the first
Man that knew anything I happened in with.
I'll ask you later—don't let me forget it.'

The Doctor looked at Lafe and looked away.
A man? A brute. Naked above the waist,
He sat there creased and shining in the light,
Fumbling the buttons in a well-starched shirt.
'I'm moving into a size-larger shirt.
I've felt mean lately; mean's no name for it.
I just found what the matter was tonight:
I've been a-choking like a nursery tree
When it outgrows the wire band of its name tag.
I blamed it on the hot spell we've been having.
'Twas nothing but my foolish hanging back,
Not liking to own up I'd grown a size.
Number eighteen this is. What size do you wear?'

The Doctor caught his throat convulsively.
'Oh—ah—fourteen—fourteen.'

                              'Fourteen! You say so!
I can remember when I wore fourteen.
And come to think I must have back at home
More than a hundred collars, size fourteen.
Too bad to waste them all. You ought to have them.
They're yours and welcome; let me send them to you.
What makes you stand there on one leg like that?
You're not much furtherer than where Kike left you.
You act as if you wished you hadn't come.
Sit down or lie down, friend; you make me nervous.'

The Doctor made a subdued dash for it,
And propped himself at bay against a pillow.

'Not that way, with your shoes on Kike's white bed.
You can't rest that way. Let me pull your shoes off.'

'Don't touch me, please—I say, don't touch me, please.
I'll not be put to bed by you, my man.'

'Just as you say. Have it your own way then.
"My man" is it? You talk like a professor.
Speaking of who's afraid of who, however,
I'm thinking I have more to lose than you
If anything should happen to be wrong.
Who wants to cut your number fourteen throat!
Let's have a showdown as an evidence
Of good faith. There is ninety dollars.
Come, if you're not afraid.'

      'I'm not afraid.
There's five: that's all I carry.'

       'I can search you?
Where are you moving over to? Stay still.
You'd better tuck your money under you
And sleep on it the way I always do
When I'm with people I don't trust at night.'

'Will you believe me if I put it there
Right on the counterpane—that I do trust you?'

'You'd say so, Mister Man.—I'm a collector.
My ninety isn't mine—you won't think that.
I pick it up a dollar at a time
All round the country for the *Weekly News*,
Published in Bow. You know the *Weekly News*?'

'Known it since I was young.'

      'Then you know me.
Now we are getting on together—talking.
I'm sort of Something for it at the front.
My business is to find what people want:
They pay for it, and so they ought to have it.
Fairbanks, he says to me—he's editor—
"Feel out the public sentiment"—he says.

A good deal comes on me when all is said.
The only trouble is we disagree
In politics: I'm Vermont Democrat—
You know what that is, sort of double-dyed;
The *News* has always been Republican.
Fairbanks, he says to me, "Help us this year,"
Meaning by us their ticket. "No," I says,
"I can't and won't. You've been in long enough:
It's time you turned around and boosted us.
You'll have to pay me more than ten a week
If I'm expected to elect Bill Taft.
I doubt if I could do it anyway." '

'You seem to shape the paper's policy.'

'You see I'm in with everybody, know 'em all.
I almost know their farms as well as they do.'

'You drive around? It must be pleasant work.'

'It's business, but I can't say it's not fun.
What I like best's the lay of different farms,
Coming out on them from a stretch of woods,
Or over a hill or round a sudden corner.
I like to find folks getting out in spring,
Raking the dooryard, working near the house.
Later they get out further in the fields.
Everything's shut sometimes except the barn;
The family's all away in some back meadow.
There's a hay load a-coming—when it comes.
And later still they all get driven in:
The fields are stripped to lawn, the garden patches
Stripped to bare ground, the maple trees
To whips and poles. There's nobody about.
The chimney, though, keeps up a good brisk smoking.
And I lie back and ride. I take the reins

Only when someone's coming, and the mare
Stops when she likes: I tell her when to go.
I've spoiled Jemima in more ways than one.
She's got so she turns in at every house
As if she had some sort of curvature,
No matter if I have no errand there.
She thinks I'm sociable. I maybe am.
It's seldom I get down except for meals, though.
Folks entertain me from the kitchen doorstep,
All in a family row down to the youngest.'

'One would suppose they might not be as glad
To see you as you are to see them.'

                                    'Oh,
Because I want their dollar? I don't want
Anything they've not got. I never dun.
I'm there, and they can pay me if they like.
I go nowhere on purpose: I happen by.
Sorry there is no cup to give you a drink.
I drink out of the bottle—not your style.
Mayn't I offer you—?'

                            'No, no no, thank you.'

'Just as you say. Here's looking at you then.—
And now I'm leaving you a little while.
You'll rest easier when I'm gone, perhaps—
Lie down—let yourself go and get some sleep.
But first—let's see—what was I going to ask you?
Those collars—who shall I address them to,
Suppose you aren't awake when I come back?'

'Really, friend, I can't let you. You—may need them.'

'Not till I shrink, when they'll be out of style.'

'But really I—I have so many collars.'

'I don't know who I rather would have have them.
They're only turning yellow where they are.
But you're the doctor as the saying is.
I'll put the light out. Don't you wait for me:
I've just begun the night. You get some sleep.
I'll knock so-fashion and peep round the door
When I come back so you'll know who it is.
There's nothing I'm afraid of like scared people.
I don't want you should shoot me in the head.
What am I doing carrying off this bottle?
There now, you get some sleep.'

                    He shut the door.
The Doctor slid a little down the pillow.

nature poems—ironic
dialogue—much less so

HOME BURIAL

He saw her from the bottom of the stairs
Before she saw him. She was starting down,
Looking back over her shoulder at some fear.
She took a doubtful step and then undid it
To raise herself and look again. He spoke
Advancing toward her: 'What is it you see
From up there always—for I want to know.'
She turned and sank upon her skirts at that,
And her face changed from terrified to dull.
He said to gain time: 'What is it you see,'
Mounting until she cowered under him.
'I will find out now—you must tell me, dear.'
She, in her place, refused him any help
With the least stiffening of her neck and silence.
She let him look, sure that he wouldn't see,

sexual
act

male
domination

man—practical
woman—romantic

41

Blind creature; and awhile he didn't see.
But at last he murmured. 'Oh,' and again, 'Oh.'

'What is it—what?' she said.

        'Just that I see.'

'You don't,' she challenged. 'Tell me what it is.'

'The wonder is I didn't see at once.
I never noticed it from here before.
I must be wonted to it—that's the reason.
The little graveyard where my people are!
So small the window frames the whole of it.
Not so much larger than a bedroom, is it?
There are three stones of slate and one of marble,
Broad-shouldered little slabs there in the sunlight
On the sidehill. We haven't to mind *those*.
But I understand: it is not the stones,
But the child's mound—'

     'Don't, don't, don't, don't,' she cried.

She withdrew shrinking from beneath his arm
That rested on the bannister, and slid downstairs;
And turned on him with such a daunting look,
He said twice over before he knew himself:
'Can't a man speak of his own child he's lost?'

'Not you! Oh, where's my hat? Oh, I don't need it!
I must get out of here. I must get air.
I don't know rightly whether any man can.'

'Amy! Don't go to someone else this time.
Listen to me. I won't come down the stairs.'
He sat and fixed his chin between his fists.
'There's something I should like to ask you, dear.'

'You don't know how to ask it.'

Home Burial

> 'Help me, then.'

Her fingers moved the latch for all reply.

'My words are nearly always an offense.
I don't know how to speak of anything
So as to please you. But I might be taught
I should suppose. I can't say I see how.
A man must partly give up being a man
With women-folk. We could have some arrangement
By which I'd bind myself to keep hands off
Anything special you're a-mind to name.
Though I don't like such things 'twixt those that love.
Two that don't love can't live together without them.
But two that do can't live together with them.'
She moved the latch a little. 'Don't—don't go.
Don't carry it to someone else this time.
Tell me about it if it's something human.
Let me into your grief. I'm not so much
Unlike other folks as your standing there
Apart would make me out. Give me my chance.
I do think, though, you overdo it a little.
What was it brought you up to think it the thing
To take your mother-loss of a first child
So inconsolably—in the face of love.
You'd think his memory might be satisfied—'

'There you go sneering now!'

> 'I'm not, I'm not!
You make me angry. I'll come down to you.
God, what a woman! And it's come to this,
A man can't speak of his own child that's dead.'

'You can't because you don't know how to speak.
If you had any feelings, you that dug

With your own hand—how could you?—his little grave;
I saw you from that very window there,
Making the gravel leap and leap in air,
Leap up, like that, like that, and land so lightly
And roll back down the mound beside the hole.
I thought, Who is that man? I didn't know you.
And I crept down the stairs and up the stairs
To look again, and still your spade kept lifting.
Then you came in. I heard your rumbling voice
Out in the kitchen, and I don't know why,
But I went near to see with my own eyes.
You could sit there with the stains on your shoes
Of the fresh earth from your own baby's grave
And talk about your everyday concerns.
You had stood the spade up against the wall
Outside there in the entry, for I saw it.'

'I shall laugh the worst laugh I ever laughed.
I'm cursed. God, if I don't believe I'm cursed.'

'I can repeat the very words you were saying.
"Three foggy mornings and one rainy day
Will rot the best birch fence a man can build."
Think of it, talk like that at such a time!
What had how long it takes a birch to rot
To do with what was in the darkened parlor.
You *couldn't* care! The nearest friends can go
With anyone to death, comes so far short
They might as well not try to go at all.
No, from the time when one is sick to death,
One is alone, and he dies more alone.
Friends make pretense of following to the grave,
But before one is in it, their minds are turned
And making the best of their way back to life
And living people, and things they understand.

But the world's evil. I won't have grief so
If I can change it. Oh, I won't, I won't!'

'There, you have said it all and you feel better.
You won't go now. You're crying. Close the door.
The heart's gone out of it: why keep it up.
Amy! There's someone coming down the road!'

'*You*—oh, you think the talk is all. I must go—
Somewhere out of this house. How can I make you—'

'If—you—do!' She was opening the door wider.
'Where do you mean to go? First tell me that.
I'll follow and bring you back by force. I *will!*—'

THE BLACK COTTAGE

We chanced in passing by that afternoon
To catch it in a sort of special picture
Among tar-banded ancient cherry trees,
Set well back from the road in rank lodged grass,
The little cottage we were speaking of,
A front with just a door between two windows,
Fresh painted by the shower a velvet black.
We paused, the minister and I, to look.
He made as if to hold it at arm's length
Or put the leaves aside that framed it in.
'Pretty,' he said. 'Come in. No one will care.'
The path was a vague parting in the grass
That led us to a weathered window-sill.
We pressed our faces to the pane. 'You see,' he said,
'Everything's as she left it when she died.
Her sons won't sell the house or the things in it.
They say they mean to come and summer here
Where they were boys. They haven't come this year.

They live so far away—one is out west—
It will be hard for them to keep their word.
Anyway they won't have the place disturbed.'
A buttoned hair-cloth lounge spread scrolling arms
Under a crayon portrait on the wall,
Done sadly from an old daguerreotype.
'That was the father as he went to war.
She always, when she talked about the war,
Sooner or later came and leaned, half knelt
Against the lounge beside it, though I doubt
If such unlifelike lines kept power to stir
Anything in her after all the years.
He fell at Gettysburg or Fredericksburg,
I ought to know—it makes a difference which:
Fredericksburg wasn't Gettysburg, of course.
But what I'm getting to is how forsaken
A little cottage this has always seemed;
Since she went more than ever, but before—
I don't mean altogether by the lives
That had gone out of it, the father first,
Then the two sons, till she was left alone.
(Nothing could draw her after those two sons.
She valued the considerate neglect
She had at some cost taught them after years.)
I mean by the world's having passed it by—
As we almost got by this afternoon.
It always seems to me a sort of mark
To measure how far fifty years have brought us.
Why not sit down if you are in no haste?
These doorsteps seldom have a visitor.
The warping boards pull out their own old nails
With none to tread and put them in their place.
She had her own idea of things, the old lady.
And she liked talk. She had seen Garrison

And Whittier, and had her story of them.
One wasn't long in learning that she thought
Whatever else the Civil War was for,
It wasn't just to keep the States together,
Nor just to free the slaves, though it did both.
She wouldn't have believed those ends enough
To have given outright for them all she gave.
Her giving somehow touched the principle
That all men are created free and equal.
And to hear her quaint phrases—so removed
From the world's view today of all those things.
That's a hard mystery of Jefferson's.
What did he mean? Of course the easy way
Is to decide it simply isn't true.
It may not be. I heard a fellow say so.
But never mind, the Welshman got it planted
Where it will trouble us a thousand years.
Each age will have to reconsider it.
You couldn't tell her what the West was saying,
And what the South to her serene belief.
She had some art of hearing and yet not
Hearing the latter wisdom of the world.
White was the only race she ever knew.
Black she had scarcely seen, and yellow never.
But how could they be made so very unlike
By the same hand working in the same stuff?
She had supposed the war decided that.
What are you going to do with such a person?
Strange how such innocence gets its own way.
I shouldn't be surprised if in this world
It were the force that would at last prevail.
Do you know but for her there was a time
When to please younger members of the church,
Or rather say non-members in the church,

Whom we all have to think of nowadays,
I would have changed the Creed a very little?
Not that she ever had to ask me not to;
It never got so far as that; but the bare thought
Of her old tremulous bonnet in the pew,
And of her half asleep was too much for me.
Why, I might wake her up and startle her.
It was the words "descended into Hades"
That seemed too pagan to our liberal youth.
You know they suffered from a general onslaught.
And well, if they weren't true why keep right on
Saying them like the heathen? We could drop them.
Only—there was the bonnet in the pew.
Such a phrase couldn't have meant much to her.
But suppose she had missed it from the Creed
As a child misses the unsaid Good-night,
And falls asleep with heartache—how should *I* feel?
I'm just as glad she made me keep hands off,
For, dear me, why abandon a belief
Merely because it ceases to be true.
Cling to it long enough, and not a doubt
It will turn true again, for so it goes.
Most of the change we think we see in life
Is due to truths being in and out of favor.
As I sit here, and oftentimes, I wish
I could be monarch of a desert land
I could devote and dedicate forever
To the truths we keep coming back and back to.
So desert it would have to be, so walled
By mountain ranges half in summer snow,
No one would covet it or think it worth
The pains of conquering to force change on.
Scattered oases where men dwelt, but mostly
Sand dunes held loosely in tamarisk

Blown over and over themselves in idleness.
Sand grains should sugar in the natal dew
The babe born to the desert, the sand storm
Retard mid-waste my cowering caravans—
There are bees in this wall.' He struck the clapboards,
Fierce heads looked out; small bodies pivoted.
We rose to go. Sunset blazed on the windows.

BLUEBERRIES

'You ought to have seen what I saw on my way
To the village, through Patterson's pasture today:
Blueberries as big as the end of your thumb,
Real sky-blue, and heavy, and ready to drum
In the cavernous pail of the first one to come!
And all ripe together, not some of them green
And some of them ripe! You ought to have seen!'

'I don't know what part of the pasture you mean.'

'You know where they cut off the woods—let me see—
It was two years ago—or no!—can it be
No longer than that?—and the following fall
The fire ran and burned it all up but the wall.'

'Why, there hasn't been time for the bushes to grow.
That's always the way with the blueberries, though:
There may not have been the ghost of a sign
Of them anywhere under the shade of the pine,
But get the pine out of the way, you may burn
The pasture all over until not a fern
Or grass-blade is left, not to mention a stick,
And presto, they're up all around you as thick
And hard to explain as a conjuror's trick.'

'It must be on charcoal they fatten their fruit.
I taste in them sometimes the flavor of soot.
And after all really they're ebony skinned:
The blue's but a mist from the breath of the wind,
A tarnish that goes at a touch of the hand,
And less than the tan with which pickers are tanned.'

'Does Patterson know what he has, do you think?'

'He may and not care and so leave the chewink
To gather them for him—you know what he is.
He won't make the fact that they're rightfully his
An excuse for keeping us other folk out.'

'I wonder you didn't see Loren about.'

'The best of it was that I did. Do you know,
I was just getting through what the field had to show
And over the wall and into the road,
When who should come by, with a democrat-load
Of all the young chattering Lorens alive,
But Loren, the fatherly, out for a drive.'

'He saw you, then? What did he do? Did he frown?'

'He just kept nodding his head up and down.
You know how politely he always goes by.
But he thought a big thought—I could tell by his eye—
Which being expressed, might be this in effect:
"I have left those there berries, I shrewdly suspect,
To ripen too long. I am greatly to blame." '

'He's a thriftier person than some I could name.'

'He seems to be thrifty; and hasn't he need,
With the mouths of all those young Lorens to feed?
He has brought them all up on wild berries, they say,
Like birds. They store a great many away.

They eat them the year round, and those they don't eat
They sell in the store and buy shoes for their feet.'

'Who cares what they say? It's a nice way to live,
Just taking what Nature is willing to give,
Not forcing her hand with harrow and plow.'

'I wish you had seen his perpetual bow—
And the air of the youngsters! No one of them turned,
And they looked so solemn-absurdly concerned.'

'I wish I knew half what the flock of them know
Of where all the berries and other things grow,
Cranberries in bogs and raspberries on top
Of the boulder-strewn mountain, and when they will crop.
I met them one day and each had a flower
Stuck into his berries as fresh as a shower;
Some strange kind—they told me it hadn't a name.'

'I've told you how once not long after we came,
I almost provoked poor Loren to mirth
By going to him of all people on earth
To ask if he knew any fruit to be had
For the picking. The rascal, he said he'd be glad
To tell if he knew. But the year had been bad.
There *had* been some berries—but those were all gone.
He didn't say where they had been. He went on:
"I'm sure—I'm sure"—as polite as could be.
He spoke to his wife in the door, "Let me see,
Mame, *we* don't know any good berrying place?"
It was all he could do to keep a straight face.'

'If he thinks all the fruit that grows wild is for him,
He'll find he's mistaken. See here, for a whim,
We'll pick in the Pattersons' pasture this year.
We'll go in the morning, that is, if it's clear,
And the sun shines out warm: the vines must be wet.

It's so long since I picked I almost forget
How we used to pick berries: we took one look round
Then sank out of sight like trolls underground,
And saw nothing more of each other, or heard,
Unless when you said I was keeping a bird
Away from its nest, and I said it was you.
"Well, one of us is." For complaining it flew
Around and around us. And then for a while
We picked, till I feared you had wandered a mile,
And I thought I had lost you. I lifted a shout
Too loud for the distance you were, it turned out,
For when you made answer, your voice was as low
As talking—you stood up beside me, you know.'

'We sha'n't have the place to ourselves to enjoy—
Not likely, when all the young Lorens deploy.
They'll be there tomorrow, or even tonight.
They won't be too friendly—they may be polite—
To people they look on as having no right
To pick where they're picking. But we won't complain.
You ought to have seen how it looked in the rain,
The fruit mixed with water in layers of leaves,
Like two kinds of jewels, a vision for thieves.'

AFTER APPLE-PICKING

My long two-pointed ladder's sticking through a tree
Toward heaven still,
And there's a barrel that I didn't fill
Beside it, and there may be two or three
Apples I didn't pick upon some bough.
But I am done with apple-picking now.
Essence of winter sleep is on the night,
The scent of apples: I am drowsing off.

After Apple-Picking

I cannot rub the strangeness from my sight
I got from looking through a pane of glass
I skimmed this morning from the drinking trough
And held against the world of hoary grass.
It melted, and I let it fall and break.
But I was well
Upon my way to sleep before it fell,
And I could tell
What form my dreaming was about to take.
Magnified apples appear and disappear,
Stem end and blossom end,
And every fleck of russet showing clear.
My instep arch not only keeps the ache,
It keeps the pressure of a ladder-round.
I feel the ladder sway as the boughs bend.
And I keep hearing from the cellar bin
The rumbling sound
Of load on load of apples coming in.
For I have had too much
Of apple-picking: I am overtired
Of the great harvest I myself desired.
There were ten thousand thousand fruit to touch,
Cherish in hand, lift down, and not let fall.
For all
That struck the earth,
No matter if not bruised or spiked with stubble,
Went surely to the cider-apple heap
As of no worth.
One can see what will trouble
This sleep of mine, whatever sleep it is.
Were he not gone,
The woodchuck could say whether it's like his
Long sleep, as I describe its coming on,
Or just some human sleep.

THE CODE

There were three in the meadow by the brook
Gathering up windrows, piling cocks of hay,
With an eye always lifted toward the west
Where an irregular sun-bordered cloud
Darkly advanced with a perpetual dagger
Flickering across its bosom. Suddenly
One helper, thrusting pitchfork in the ground,
Marched himself off the field and home. One stayed.
The town-bred farmer failed to understand.

'What is there wrong?'

                    'Something you just now said.'

'What did I say?'

                'About our taking pains.'

'To cock the hay?—because it's going to shower?
I said that more than half an hour ago.
I said it to myself as much as you.'

'You didn't know. But James is one big fool.
He thought you meant to find fault with his work.
That's what the average farmer would have meant.
James would take time, of course, to chew it over
Before he acted: he's just got round to act.'

'He is a fool if that's the way he takes me.'

'Don't let it bother you. You've found out something.
The hand that knows his business won't be told
To do work better or faster—those two things.
I'm as particular as anyone:
Most likely I'd have served you just the same.
But I know you don't understand our ways.

The Code

You were just talking what was in your mind,
What was in all our minds, and you weren't hinting.
Tell you a story of what happened once:
I was up here in Salem at a man's
Named Sanders with a gang of four or five
Doing the haying. No one liked the boss.
He was one of the kind sports call a spider,
All wiry arms and legs that spread out wavy
From a humped body nigh as big's a biscuit
But work! that man could work, especially
If by so doing he could get more work
Out of his hired help. I'm not denying
He was hard on himself. I couldn't find
That he kept any hours—not for himself.
Daylight and lantern-light were one to him:
I've heard him pounding in the barn all night.
But what he liked was someone to encourage.
Them that he couldn't lead he'd get behind
And drive, the way you can, you know, in mowing—
Keep at their heels and threaten to mow their legs off.
I'd seen about enough of his bulling tricks
(We call that bulling). I'd been watching him.
So when he paired off with me in the hayfield
To load the load, thinks I, Look out for trouble.
I built the load and topped it off; old Sanders
Combed it down with a rake and says, "O.K."
Everything went well till we reached the barn
With a big jag to empty in a bay.
You understand that meant the easy job
For the man up on top of throwing *down*
The hay and rolling it off wholesale,
Where on a mow it would have been slow lifting.
You wouldn't think a fellow'd need much urging
Under those circumstances, would you now?

But the old fool seizes his fork in both hands,
And looking up bewhiskered out of the pit,
Shouts like an army captain, "Let her come!"
Thinks I, D'ye mean it? "What was that you said?"
I asked out loud, so's there'd be no mistake,
"Did you say, Let her come?" "Yes, let her come."
He said it over, but he said it softer.
Never you say a thing like that to a man,
Not if he values what he is. God, I'd as soon
Murdered him as left out his middle name.
I'd built the load and knew right where to find it.
Two or three forkfuls I picked lightly round for
Like meditating, and then I just dug in
And dumped the rackful on him in ten lots.
I looked over the side once in the dust
And caught sight of him treading-water-like,
Keeping his head above. "Damn ye," I says,
"That gets ye!" He squeaked like a squeezed rat.
That was the last I saw or heard of him.
I cleaned the rack and drove out to cool off.
As I sat mopping hayseed from my neck,
And sort of waiting to be asked about it,
One of the boys sings out, "Where's the old man?"
"I left him in the barn under the hay.
If ye want him, ye can go and dig him out."
They realized from the way I swabbed my neck
More than was needed something must be up.
They headed for the barn; I stayed where I was.
They told me afterward. First they forked hay,
A lot of it, out into the barn floor.
Nothing! They listened for him. Not a rustle.
I guess they thought I'd spiked him in the temple
Before I buried him, or I couldn't have managed.
They excavated more. "Go keep his wife

Out of the barn." Someone looked in a window,
And curse me if he wasn't in the kitchen
Slumped way down in a chair, with both his feet
Against the stove, the hottest day that summer.
He looked so clean disgusted from behind
There was no one that dared to stir him up,
Or let him know that he was being looked at.
Apparently I hadn't buried him
(I may have knocked him down); but my just trying
To bury him had hurt his dignity.
He had gone to the house so's not to meet me.
He kept away from us all afternoon.
We tended to his hay. We saw him out
After a while picking peas in his garden:
He couldn't keep away from doing something.'

'Weren't you relieved to find he wasn't dead?'

'No! and yet I don't know—it's hard to say.
I went about to kill him fair enough.'

'You took an awkward way. Did he discharge you?'

'Discharge me? No! He knew I did just right.'

THE GENERATIONS OF MEN

A governor it was proclaimed this time,
When all who would come seeking in New Hampshire
Ancestral memories might come together.
And those of the name Stark gathered in Bow,
A rock-strewn town where farming has fallen off,
And sprout-lands flourish where the ax has gone.
Someone had literally run to earth
In an old cellar hole in a by-road

The origin of all the family there.
Thence they were sprung, so numerous a tribe
That now not all the houses left in town
Made shift to shelter them without the help
Of here and there a tent in grove and orchard.
They were at Bow, but that was not enough:
Nothing would do but they must fix a day
To stand together on the crater's verge
That turned them on the world, and try to fathom
The past and get some strangeness out of it.
But rain spoiled all. The day began uncertain,
With clouds low trailing and moments of rain that misted.
The young folk held some hope out to each other
Till well toward noon when the storm settled down
With a swish in the grass. 'What if the others
Are there,' they said. 'It isn't going to rain.'
Only one from a farm not far away
Strolled thither, not expecting he would find
Anyone else, but out of idleness.
One, and one other, yes, for there were two.
The second round the curving hillside road
Was a girl; and she halted some way off
To reconnoiter, and then made up her mind
At least to pass by and see who he was,
And perhaps hear some word about the weather.
This was some Stark she didn't know. He nodded.
'No fête today,' he said.

                    'It looks that way.'

She swept the heavens, turning on her heel.
'I only idled down.'

                    'I idled down.'

Provision there had been for just such meeting

The Generations of Men

Of stranger cousins, in a family tree
Drawn on a sort of passport with the branch
Of the one bearing it done in detail—
Some zealous one's laborious device.
She made a sudden movement toward her bodice,
As one who clasps her heart. They laughed together.
'Stark?' he inquired. 'No matter for the proof.'

'Yes, Stark. And you?'

      'I'm Stark.' He drew his passport.

'You know we might not be and still be cousins:
The town is full of Chases, Lowes, and Baileys,
All claiming some priority in Starkness.
My mother was a Lane, yet might have married
Anyone upon earth and still her children
Would have been Starks, and doubtless here today.'

'You riddle with your genealogy
Like a Viola. I don't follow you.'

'I only mean my mother was a Stark
Several times over, and by marrying father
No more than brought us back into the name.'

'One ought not to be thrown into confusion
By a plain statement of relationship,
But I own what you say makes my head spin.
You take my card—you seem so good at such things—
And see if you can reckon our cousinship.
Why not take seats here on the cellar wall
And dangle feet among the raspberry vines?'

'Under the shelter of the family tree.'

'Just so—that ought to be enough protection.'

'Not from the rain. I think it's going to rain.'

'It's raining.'

    'No, it's misting; let's be fair.
Does the rain seem to you to cool the eyes?'

The situation was like this: the road
Bowed outward on the mountain halfway up,
And disappeared and ended not far off.
No one went home that way. The only house
Beyond where they were was a shattered seedpod.
And below roared a brook hidden in trees,
The sound of which was silence for the place.
This he sat listening to till she gave judgment.

'On father's side, it seems, we're—let me see—'

'Don't be too technical.—You have three cards.'

'Four cards, one yours, three mine, one for each branch
Of the Stark family I'm a member of.'

'D'you know a person so related to herself
Is supposed to be mad.'

     'I may be mad.'

'You look so, sitting out here in the rain
Studying genealogy with me
You never saw before. What will we come to
With all this pride of ancestry, we Yankees?
I think we're all mad. Tell me why we're here
Drawn into town about this cellar hole
Like wild geese on a lake before a storm?
What do we see in such a hole, I wonder.'

'The Indians had a myth of Chicamoztoc,
Which means The Seven Caves that We Came out of.
This is the pit from which we Starks were digged.'

'You must be learned. That's what you see in it?'

'And what do you see?'

                    'Yes, what *do* I see?
First let me look. I see raspberry vines—'

'Oh, if you're going to use your eyes, just hear
What *I* see. It's a little, little boy,
As pale and dim as a match flame in the sun;
He's groping in the cellar after jam,
He thinks it's dark and it's flooded with daylight.'

'He's nothing. Listen. When I lean like this
I can make out old Grandsir Stark distinctly,—
With his pipe in his mouth and his brown jug—
Bless you, it isn't Grandsir Stark, it's Granny,
But the pipe's there and smoking and the jug.
She's after cider, the old girl, she's thirsty;
Here's hoping she gets her drink and gets out safely.'

'Tell me about her. Does she look like me?'

'She should, shouldn't she, you're so many times
Over descended from her. I believe
She does look like you. Stay the way you are.
The nose is just the same, and so's the chin—
Making allowance, making due allowance.'

'You poor, dear, great, great, great, great Granny!'

'See that you get her greatness right. Don't stint her.'

'Yes, it's important, though you think it isn't.
I won't be teased. But see how wet I am.'

'Yes, you must go; we can't stay here for ever.
But wait until I give you a hand up.
A bead of silver water more or less

Strung on your hair won't hurt your summer looks.
I wanted to try something with the noise
That the brook raises in the empty valley.
We have seen visions—now consult the voices.
Something I must have learned riding in trains
When I was young. I used to use the roar
To set the voices speaking out of it,
Speaking or singing, and the band-music playing.
Perhaps you have the art of what I mean.
I've never listened in among the sounds
That a brook makes in such a wild descent.
It ought to give a purer oracle.'

'It's as you throw a picture on a screen:
The meaning of it all is out of you;
The voices give you what you wish to hear.'

'Strangely, it's anything they wish to give.'

'Then I don't know. It must be strange enough.
I wonder if it's not your make-believe.
What do you think you're like to hear today?'

'From the sense of our having been together—
But why take time for what I'm like to hear?
I'll tell you what the voices really say.
You will do very well right where you are
A little longer. I mustn't feel too hurried,
Or I can't give myself to hear the voices.'

'Is this some trance you are withdrawing into?'

'You must be very still; you mustn't talk.'

'I'll hardly breathe.'

                'The voices seem to say—'

'I'm waiting.'

   'Don't! The voices seem to say:
Call her Nausicaä, the unafraid
Of an acquaintance made adventurously.'

'I let you say that—on consideration.'

'I don't see very well how you can help it.
You want the truth. I speak but by the voices.
You see they know I haven't had your name,
Though what a name should matter between us—'

'I shall suspect—'

   'Be good. The voices say:
Call her Nausicaä, and take a timber
That you shall find lies in the cellar charred
Among the raspberries, and hew and shape it
For a door-sill or other corner piece
In a new cottage on the ancient spot.
The life is not yet all gone out of it.
And come and make your summer dwelling here,
And perhaps she will come, still unafraid,
And sit before you in the open door
With flowers in her lap until they fade,
But not come in across the sacred sill—'

'I wonder where your oracle is tending.
You can see that there's something wrong with it,
Or it would speak in dialect. Whose voice
Does it purport to speak in? Not old Grandsir's
Nor Granny's, surely. Call up one of them.
They have best right to be heard in this place.'

'You seem so partial to our great-grandmother
(Nine times removed. Correct me if I err.)

You will be likely to regard as sacred
Anything she may say. But let me warn you,
Folks in her day were given to plain speaking.
You think you'd best tempt her at such a time?'

'It rests with us always to cut her off.'

'Well then, it's Granny speaking: "I dunnow!
Mebbe I'm wrong to take it as I do.
There ain't no names quite like the old ones though,
Nor never will be to my way of thinking.
One mustn't bear too hard on the newcomers,
But there's a dite too many of them for comfort.
I should feel easier if I could see
More of the salt wherewith they're to be salted.
Son, you do as you're told! You take the timber—
It's as sound as the day when it was cut—
And begin over—" There, she'd better stop.
You can see what is troubling Granny, though.
But don't you think we sometimes make too much
Of the old stock? What counts is the ideals,
And those will bear some keeping still about.'

'I can see we are going to be good friends.'

'I like your "going to be." You said just now
It's going to rain.'

             'I know, and it was raining.
I let you say all that. But I must go now.'

'You let me say it? on consideration?
How shall we say good-by in such a case?'

'How shall we?'

             'Will you leave the way to me?'

'No, I don't trust your eyes. You've said enough.

Now give me your hand up.—Pick me that flower.'

'Where shall we meet again?'

'Nowhere but here
Once more before we meet elsewhere.'

'In rain?'

'It ought to be in rain. Sometime in rain.
In rain tomorrow, shall we, if it rains?
But if we must, in sunshine.' So she went.

THE FEAR

A lantern light from deeper in the barn
Shone on a man and woman in the door
And threw their lurching shadows on a house
Nearby, all dark in every glossy window.
A horse's hoof pawed once the hollow floor,
And the back of the gig they stood beside
Moved in a little. The man grasped a wheel,
The woman spoke out sharply, 'Whoa, stand still!
I saw it just as plain as a white plate,'
She said, 'as the light on the dashboard ran
Along the bushes at the roadside—a man's face.
You *must* have seen it too.'

'I didn't see it.
Are you sure—'

'Yes, I'm sure!'

'—it was a face?'

'Joel, I'll have to look. I can't go in,
I can't, and leave a thing like that unsettled.

65

Doors locked and curtains drawn will make no difference.
I always have felt strange when we came home
To the dark house after so long an absence,
And the key rattled loudly into place
Seemed to warn someone to be getting out
At one door as we entered at another.
What if I'm right, and someone all the time—
Don't hold my arm!'

     'I say it's someone passing.'

'You speak as if this were a traveled road.
You forget where we are. What is beyond
That he'd be going to or coming from
At such an hour of night, and on foot too?
What was he standing still for in the bushes?'

'It's not so very late—it's only dark.
There's more in it than you're inclined to say.
Did he look like—?'

      'He looked like anyone.
I'll never rest tonight unless I know.
Give me the lantern.'

     'You don't want the lantern.'

She pushed past him and got it for herself.

'You're not to come,' she said. 'This is my business
If the time's come to face it, I'm the one
To put it the right way. He'd never dare—
Listen! He kicked a stone. Hear that, hear that!
He's coming towards us. Joel, *go* in—please.
Hark!—I don't hear him now. But please go in.'

'In the first place you can't make me believe it's—'

The Fear

'It is—or someone else he's sent to watch.
And now's the time to have it out with him
While we know definitely where he is.
Let him get off and he'll be everywhere
Around us, looking out of trees and bushes
Till I sha'n't dare to set a foot outdoors.
And I can't stand it. Joel, let me go!'

'But it's nonsense to think he'd care enough.'

'You mean you couldn't understand his caring.
Oh, but you see he hadn't had enough—
Joel, I won't—I won't—I promise you.
We mustn't say hard things. You mustn't either.'

'I'll be the one, if anybody goes!
But you give him the advantage with this light.
What couldn't he do to us standing here!
And if to see was what he wanted, why,
He has seen all there was to see and gone.'

He appeared to forget to keep his hold,
But advanced with her as she crossed the grass.

'What do you want?' she cried to all the dark.
She stretched up tall to overlook the light
That hung in both hands hot against her skirt.

'There's no one; so you're wrong,' he said.

                                        'There is.—
What do you want?' she cried, and then herself
Was startled when an answer really came.

'Nothing.' It came from well along the road.

She reached a hand to Joel for support:
The smell of scorching woolen made her faint.
'What are you doing round this house at night?'

'Nothing.' A pause: there seemed no more to say.

And then the voice again: 'You seem afraid.
I saw by the way you whipped up the horse.
I'll just come forward in the lantern light
And let you see.'

    'Yes, do.—Joel, go back!'

She stood her ground against the noisy steps
That came on, but her body rocked a little.

'You see,' the voice said.

      'Oh.' She looked and looked.

'You don't see—I've a child here by the hand.
A robber wouldn't have his family with him.'

'What's a child doing at this time of night—?'

'Out walking. Every child should have the memory
Of at least one long-after-bedtime walk.
What, son?'

'Then I should think you'd try to find
Somewhere to walk—'

     'The highway, as it happens—
We're stopping for the fortnight down at Dean's.'

'But if that's all—Joel—you realize—
You won't think anything. You understand?
You understand that we have to be careful.
This is a very, very lonely place.
Joel!' She spoke as if she couldn't turn.
The swinging lantern lengthened to the ground,
It touched, it struck, it clattered and went out.

THE WOOD-PILE

Out walking in the frozen swamp one gray day,
I paused and said, 'I will turn back from here.
No, I will go on farther—and we shall see.'
The hard snow held me, save where now and then
One foot went through. The view was all in lines
Straight up and down of tall slim trees
Too much alike to mark or name a place by
So as to say for certain I was here
Or somewhere else: I was just far from home.
A small bird flew before me. He was careful
To put a tree between us when he lighted,
And say no word to tell me who he was
Who was so foolish as to think what *he* thought.
He thought that I was after him for a feather—
The white one in his tail; like one who takes
Everything said as personal to himself.
One flight out sideways would have undeceived him.
And then there was a pile of wood for which
I forgot him and let his little fear
Carry him off the way I might have gone,
Without so much as wishing him good-night.
He went behind it to make his last stand.
It was a cord of maple, cut and split
And piled—and measured, four by four by eight.
And not another like it could I see.
No runner tracks in this year's snow looped near it.
And it was older sure than this year's cutting,
Or even last year's or the year's before.
The wood was gray and the bark warping off it
And the pile somewhat sunken. Clematis
Had wound strings round and round it like a bundle.

What held it though on one side was a tree
Still growing, and on one a stake and prop,
These latter about to fall. I thought that only
Someone who lived in turning to fresh tasks
Could so forget his handiwork on which
He spent himself, the labor of his ax,
And leave it there far from a useful fireplace
To warm the frozen swamp as best it could
With the slow smokeless burning of decay.

Mountain Interval

THE ROAD NOT TAKEN

Two roads diverged in a yellow wood,
And sorry I could not travel both
And be one traveler, long I stood
And looked down one as far as I could
To where it bent in the undergrowth;

Then took the other, as just as fair,
And having perhaps the better claim,
Because it was grassy and wanted wear;
Though as for that the passing there
Had worn them really about the same,

And both that morning equally lay
In leaves no step had trodden black.
Oh, I kept the first for another day!
Yet knowing how way leads on to way,
I doubted if I should ever come back

I shall be telling this with a sigh
Somewhere ages and ages hence:
Two roads diverged in a wood, and I—
I took the one less traveled by,
And that has made all the difference.

CHRISTMAS TREES

A CHRISTMAS CIRCULAR LETTER

The city had withdrawn into itself
And left at last the country to the country;
When between whirls of snow not come to lie
And whirls of foliage not yet laid, there drove
A stranger to our yard, who looked the city,
Yet did in country fashion in that there
He sat and waited till he drew us out
A-buttoning coats to ask him who he was.
He proved to be the city come again
To look for something it had left behind
And could not do without and keep its Christmas.
He asked if I would sell my Christmas trees;
My woods—the young fir balsams like a place
Where houses all are churches and have spires.
I hadn't thought of them as Christmas trees.
I doubt if I was tempted for a moment
To sell them off their feet to go in cars
And leave the slope behind the house all bare,
Where the sun shines now no warmer than the moon.
I'd hate to have them know it if I was.
Yet more I'd hate to hold my trees except
As others hold theirs or refuse for them,
Beyond the time of profitable growth,

The trial by market everything must come to.
I dallied so much with the thought of selling.
Then whether from mistaken courtesy
And fear of seeming short of speech, or whether
From hope of hearing good of what was mine,
I said, 'There aren't enough to be worth while.'

'I could soon tell how many they would cut,
You let me look them over.'

                'You could look.
But don't expect I'm going to let you have them.'
Pasture they spring in, some in clumps too close
That lop each other of boughs, but not a few
Quite solitary and having equal boughs
All round and round. The latter he nodded 'Yes' to,
Or paused to say beneath some lovelier one,
With a buyer's moderation, 'That would do.'
I thought so too, but wasn't there to say so.
We climbed the pasture on the south, crossed over,
And came down on the north.

                He said, 'A thousand.'

'A thousand Christmas trees!—at what apiece?'

He felt some need of softening that to me:
'A thousand trees would come to thirty dollars.'

Then I was certain I had never meant
To let him have them. Never show surprise!
But thirty dollars seemed so small beside
The extent of pasture I should strip, three cents
(For that was all they figured out apiece),
Three cents so small beside the dollar friends
I should be writing to within the hour
Would pay in cities for good trees like those,

Regular vestry trees whole Sunday Schools
Could hang enough on to pick off enough.
A thousand Christmas trees I didn't know I had!
Worth three cents more to give away than sell
As may be shown by a simple calculation.
Too bad I couldn't lay one in a letter.
I can't help wishing I could send you one
In wishing you herewith a Merry Christmas.

AN OLD MAN'S WINTER NIGHT

All out-of-doors looked darkly in at him
Through the thin frost, almost in separate stars,
That gathers on the pane in empty rooms.
What kept his eyes from giving back the gaze
Was the lamp tilted near them in his hand.
What kept him from remembering what it was
That brought him to that creaking room was age.
He stood with barrels round him—at a loss.
And having scared the cellar under him
In clomping here, he scared it once again
In clomping off;—and scared the outer night,
Which has its sounds, familiar, like the roar
Of trees and crack of branches, common things,
But nothing so like beating on a box.
A light he was to no one but himself
Where now he sat, concerned with he knew what,
A quiet light, and then not even that.
He consigned to the moon, such as she was,
So late-arising, to the broken moon
As better than the sun in any case
For such a charge, his snow upon the roof,
His icicles along the wall to keep:

And slept. The log that shifted with a jolt
Once in the stove, disturbed him and he shifted,
And eased his heavy breathing, but still slept.
One aged man—one man—can't keep a house,
A farm, a countryside, or if he can,
It's thus he does it of a winter night.

THE TELEPHONE

'When I was just as far as I could walk
From here today,
There was an hour
All still
When leaning with my head against a flower
I heard you talk.
Don't say I didn't, for I heard you say—
You spoke from that flower on the window sill—
Do you remember what it was you said?'

'First tell me what it was you thought you heard.'

'Having found the flower and driven a bee away,
I leaned my head,
And holding by the stalk,
I listened and I thought I caught the word—
What was it? Did you call me by my name?
Or did you say—
Someone said "Come"—I heard it as I bowed.'

'I may have thought as much, but not aloud.'

'Well, so I came.'

THE OVEN BIRD

There is a singer everyone has heard,
Loud, a mid-summer and a mid-wood bird,
Who makes the solid tree trunks sound again.
He says that leaves are old and that for flowers
Mid-summer is to spring as one to ten.
He says the early petal-fall is past
When pear and cherry bloom went down in showers
On sunny days a moment overcast;
And comes that other fall we name the fall.
He says the highway dust is over all.
The bird would cease and be as other birds
But that he knows in singing not to sing.
The question that he frames in all but words
Is what to make of a diminished thing.

BOND AND FREE

Love has earth to which she clings
With hills and circling arms about—
Wall within wall to shut fear out.
But Thought has need of no such things,
For Thought has a pair of dauntless wings.

On snow and sand and turf, I see
Where Love has left a printed trace
With straining in the world's embrace.
And such is Love and glad to be.
But Thought has shaken his ankles free.

Thought cleaves the interstellar gloom
And sits in Sirius' disc all night,

Till day makes him retrace his flight,
With smell of burning on every plume,
Back past the sun to an earthly room.

His gains in heaven are what they are.
Yet some say Love by being thrall
And simply staying possesses all
In several beauty that Thought fares far
To find fused in another star.

BIRCHES

When I see birches bend to left and right
Across the lines of straighter darker trees,
I like to think some boy's been swinging them.
But swinging doesn't bend them down to stay
As ice-storms do. Often you must have seen them
Loaded with ice a sunny winter morning
After a rain. They click upon themselves
As the breeze rises, and turn many-colored
As the stir cracks and crazes their enamel.
Soon the sun's warmth makes them shed crystal shells
Shattering and avalanching on the snow-crust—
Such heaps of broken glass to sweep away
You'd think the inner dome of heaven had fallen.
They are dragged to the withered bracken by the load,
And they seem not to break; though once they are bowed
So low for long, they never right themselves:
You may see their trunks arching in the woods
Years afterwards, trailing their leaves on the ground
Like girls on hands and knees that throw their hair
Before them over their heads to dry in the sun.
But I was going to say when Truth broke in
With all her matter-of-fact about the ice-storm

I should prefer to have some boy bend them
As he went out and in to fetch the cows—
Some boy too far from town to learn baseball,
Whose only play was what he found himself,
Summer or winter, and could play alone.
One by one he subdued his father's trees
By riding them down over and over again
Until he took the stiffness out of them,
And not one but hung limp, not one was left
For him to conquer. He learned all there was
To learn about not launching out too soon
And so not carrying the tree away
Clear to the ground. He always kept his poise
To the top branches, climbing carefully
With the same pains you use to fill a cup
Up to the brim, and even above the brim.
Then he flung outward, feet first, with a swish,
Kicking his way down through the air to the ground.
So was I once myself a swinger of birches.
And so I dream of going back to be.
It's when I'm weary of considerations,
And life is too much like a pathless wood
Where your face burns and tickles with the cobwebs
Broken across it, and one eye is weeping
From a twig's having lashed across it open.
I'd like to get away from earth awhile
And then come back to it and begin over.
May no fate willfully misunderstand me
And half grant what I wish and snatch me away
Not to return. Earth's the right place for love:
I don't know where it's likely to go better.
I'd like to go by climbing a birch tree,
And climb black branches up a snow-white trunk
Toward heaven, till the tree could bear no more,

But dipped its top and set me down again.
That would be good both going and coming back.
One could do worse than be a swinger of birches.

PUTTING IN THE SEED

You come to fetch me from my work tonight
When supper's on the table, and we'll see
If I can leave off burying the white
Soft petals fallen from the apple tree
(Soft petals, yes, but not so barren quite,
Mingled with these, smooth bean and wrinkled pea;
And go along with you ere you lose sight
Of what you came for and become like me,
Slave to a springtime passion for the earth.
How Love burns through the Putting in the Seed
On through the watching for that early birth
When, just as the soil tarnishes with weed,
The sturdy seedling with arched body comes
Shouldering its way and shedding the earth crumbs.

A TIME TO TALK

When a friend calls to me from the road
And slows his horse to a meaning walk,
I don't stand still and look around
On all the hills I haven't hoed,
And shout from where I am, 'What is it?'
No, not as there is a time to talk.
I thrust my hoe in the mellow ground,
Blade-end up and five feet tall,
And plod: I go up to the stone wall
For a friendly visit.

AN ENCOUNTER

Once on the kind of day called 'weather breeder,'
When the heat slowly hazes and the sun
By its own power seems to be undone,
I was half boring through, half climbing through
A swamp of cedar. Choked with oil of cedar
And scurf of plants, and weary and over-heated,
And sorry I ever left the road I knew,
I paused and rested on a sort of hook
That had me by the coat as good as seated,
And since there was no other way to look,
Looked up toward heaven, and there against the blue,
Stood over me a resurrected tree,
A tree that had been down and raised again—
A barkless specter. He had halted too,
As if for fear of treading upon me.
I saw the strange position of his hands—
Up at his shoulders, dragging yellow strands
Of wire with something in it from men to men.
'You here?' I said. 'Where aren't you nowadays?
And what's the news you carry—if you know?
And tell me where you're off for—Montreal?
Me? I'm not off for anywhere at all.
Sometimes I wander out of beaten ways
Half looking for the orchid Calypso.'

RANGE-FINDING

The battle rent a cobweb diamond-strung
And cut a flower beside a ground bird's nest
Before it stained a single human breast.

The stricken flower bent double and so hung.
And still the bird revisited her young.
A butterfly its fall had dispossessed
A moment sought in air his flower of rest,
Then lightly stooped to it and fluttering clung.
On the bare upland pasture there had spread
O'ernight 'twixt mullein stalks a wheel of thread
And straining cables wet with silver dew.
A sudden passing bullet shook it dry.
The indwelling spider ran to greet the fly,
But finding nothing, sullenly withdrew.

THE HILL WIFE

LONELINESS

Her Word

One ought not to have to care
   So much as you and I
Care when the birds come round the house
   To seem to say good-by;

Or care so much when they come back
   With whatever it is they sing;
The truth being we are as much
   Too glad for the one thing

As we are too sad for the other here—
   With birds that fill their breasts
But with each other and themselves
   And their built or driven nests.

HOUSE FEAR

Always—I tell you this they learned—
Always at night when they returned
To the lonely house from far away
To lamps unlighted and fire gone gray,
They learned to rattle the lock and key
To give whatever might chance to be
Warning and time to be off in flight:
And preferring the out- to the in-door night,
They learned to leave the house-door wide
Until they had lit the lamp inside.

THE SMILE

Her Word

I didn't like the way he went away.
That smile! It never came of being gay.
Still he smiled—did you see him?—I was sure!
Perhaps because we gave him only bread
And the wretch knew from that that we were poor.
Perhaps because he let us give instead
Of seizing from us as he might have seized.
Perhaps he mocked at us for being wed,
Or being very young (and he was pleased
To have a vision of us old and dead).
I wonder how far down the road he's got.
He's watching from the woods as like as not.

THE OFT-REPEATED DREAM

She had no saying dark enough
    For the dark pine that kept
Forever trying the window-latch
    Of the room where they slept.

The tireless but ineffectual hands
  That with every futile pass
Made the great tree seem as a little bird
  Before the mystery of glass!

It never had been inside the room,
  And only one of the two
Was afraid in an oft-repeated dream
  Of what the tree might do.

THE IMPULSE

It was too lonely for her there,
  And too wild,
And since there were but two of them,
  And no child,

And work was little in the house,
  She was free,
And followed where he furrowed field,
  Or felled tree.

She rested on a log and tossed
  The fresh chips,
With a song only to herself
  On her lips.

And once she went to break a bough
  Of black alder.
She strayed so far she scarcely heard
  When he called her—

And didn't answer—didn't speak—
  Or return.
She stood, and then she ran and hid
  In the fern.

He never found her, though he looked
   Everywhere,
And he asked at her mother's house
   Was she there.

Sudden and swift and light as that
   The ties gave,
And he learned of finalities
   Besides the grave.

THE BONFIRE

'Oh, let's go up the hill and scare ourselves,
As reckless as the best of them tonight,
By setting fire to all the brush we piled
With pitchy hands to wait for rain or snow.
Oh, let's not wait for rain to make it safe.
The pile is ours: we dragged it bough on bough
Down dark converging paths between the pines.
Let's not care what we do with it tonight.
Divide it? No! But burn it as one pile
The way we piled it. And let's be the talk
Of people brought to windows by a light
Thrown from somewhere against their wallpaper.
Rouse them all, both the free and not so free
With saying what they'd like to do to us
For what they'd better wait till we have done.
Let's all but bring to life this old volcano,
If that is what the mountain ever was—
And scare ourselves. Let wild fire loose we will . . .

'And scare you too?' the children said together.

The Bonfire

'Why wouldn't it scare me to have a fire
Begin in smudge with ropy smoke and know
That still, if I repent, I may recall it,
But in a moment not: a little spurt
Of burning fatness, and then nothing but
The fire itself can put it out, and that
By burning out, and before it burns out
It will have roared first and mixed sparks with stars,
And sweeping round it with a flaming sword,
Made the dim trees stand back in wider circle—
Done so much and I know not how much more
I mean it shall not do if I can bind it.
Well if it doesn't with its draft bring on
A wind to blow in earnest from some quarter,
As once it did with me upon an April.
The breezes were so spent with winter blowing
They seemed to fail the bluebirds under them
Short of the perch their languid flight was toward
And my flame made a pinnacle to heaven
As I walked once around it in possession.
But the wind out of doors—you know the saying.
There came a gust. You used to think the trees
Made wind by fanning since you never knew
It blow but that you saw the trees in motion.
Something or someone watching made that gust.
It put the flame tip-down and dabbed the grass
Of over-winter with the least tip-touch
Your tongue gives salt or sugar in your hand.
The place it reached to blackened instantly.
The black was almost all there was by daylight,
That and the merest curl of cigarette smoke—
And a flame slender as the hepaticas,
Blood-root, and violets so soon to be now.
But the black spread like black death on the ground,

And I think the sky darkened with a cloud
Like winter and evening coming on together.
There were enough things to be thought of then.
Where the field stretches toward the north
And setting sun to Hyla brook, I gave it
To flames without twice thinking, where it verges
Upon the road, to flames too, though in fear
They might find fuel there, in withered brake,
Grass its full length, old silver goldenrod,
And alder and grape vine entanglement,
To leap the dusty deadline. For my own
I took what front there was beside. I knelt
And thrust hands in and held my face away.
Fight such a fire by rubbing not by beating.
A board is the best weapon if you have it.
I had my coat. And oh, I knew, I knew,
And said out loud, I couldn't bide the smother
And heat so close in; but the thought of all
The woods and town on fire by me, and all
The town turned out to fight for me—that held me.
I trusted the brook barrier, but feared
The road would fail; and on that side the fire
Died not without a noise of crackling wood—
Of something more than tinder-grass and weed—
That brought me to my feet to hold it back
By leaning back myself, as if the reins
Were round my neck and I was at the plow.
I won! But I'm sure no one ever spread
Another color over a tenth the space
That I spread coal-black over in the time
It took me. Neighbors coming home from town
Couldn't believe that so much black had come there
While they had backs turned, that it hadn't been there
When they had passed an hour or so before

Going the other way and they not seen it.
They looked about for someone to have done it.
But there was no one. I was somewhere wondering
Where all my weariness had gone and why
I walked so light on air in heavy shoes
In spite of a scorched Fourth-of-July feeling.
Why wouldn't I be scared remembering that?'

'If it scares you, what will it do to us?'

'Scare you. But if you shrink from being scared,
What would you say to war if it should come?
That's what for reasons I should like to know—
If you can comfort me by any answer.'

'Oh, but war's not for children—it's for men.'

'Now we are digging almost down to China.
My dears, my dears, you thought that—we all thought it.
So your mistake was ours. Haven't you heard, though,
About the ships where war has found them out
At sea, about the towns where war has come
Through opening clouds at night with droning speed
Further o'erhead than all but stars and angels,—
And children in the ships and in the towns?
Haven't you heard what we have lived to learn?
Nothing so new—something we had forgotten:
War is for everyone, for children too.
I wasn't going to tell you and I mustn't.
The best way is to come up hill with me
And have our fire and laugh and be afraid.'

A GIRL'S GARDEN

A neighbor of mine in the village
    Likes to tell how one spring
When she was a girl on the farm, she did
    A childlike thing.

One day she asked her father
    To give her a garden plot
To plant and tend and reap herself,
    And he said, 'Why not?'

In casting about for a corner
    He thought of an idle bit
Of walled-off ground where a shop had stood,
    And he said, 'Just it.'

And he said, 'That ought to make you
    An ideal one-girl farm,
And give you a chance to put some strength
    On your slim-jim arm.'

It was not enough of a garden,
    Her father said, to plow;
So she had to work it all by hand,
    But she don't mind now.

She wheeled the dung in the wheelbarrow
    Along a stretch of road;
But she always ran away and left
    Her not-nice load,

And hid from anyone passing.
    And then she begged the seed.
She says she thinks she planted one
    Of all things but weed.

A hill each of potatoes,
    Radishes, lettuce, peas,
Tomatoes, beets, beans, pumpkins, corn
    And even fruit trees.

And yes, she has long mistrusted
    That a cider apple tree
In bearing there today is hers,
    Or at least may be.

Her crop was a miscellany
    When all was said and done,
A little bit of everything,
    A great deal of none.

Now when she sees in the village
    How village things go,
Just when it seems to come in right,
    She says, '*I* know!

'It's as when I was a farmer—'
    Oh, never by way of advice!
And she never sins by telling the tale
    To the same person twice.

'OUT, OUT—'

The buzz saw snarled and rattled in the yard
And made dust and dropped stove-length sticks of wood,
Sweet-scented stuff when the breeze drew across it.
And from there those that lifted eyes could count
Five mountain ranges one behind the other
Under the sunset far into Vermont.

And the saw snarled and rattled, snarled and rattled,
As it ran light, or had to bear a load.
And nothing happened: day was all but done.
Call it a day, I wish they might have said
To please the boy by giving him the half hour
That a boy counts so much when saved from work.
His sister stood beside them in her apron
To tell them 'Supper.' At the word, the saw,
As if to prove saws knew what supper meant,
Leaped out at the boy's hand, or seemed to leap—
He must have given the hand. However it was,
Neither refused the meeting. But the hand!
The boy's first outcry was a rueful laugh,
As he swung toward them holding up the hand
Half in appeal, but half as if to keep
The life from spilling. Then the boy saw all—
Since he was old enough to know, big boy
Doing a man's work, though a child at heart—
He saw all spoiled. 'Don't let him cut my hand off—
The doctor, when he comes. Don't let him, sister!'
So. But the hand was gone already.
The doctor put him in the dark of ether.
He lay and puffed his lips out with his breath.
And then—the watcher at his pulse took fright.
No one believed. They listened at his heart.
Little—less—nothing!—and that ended it.
No more to build on there. And they, since they
Were not the one dead, turned to their affairs.

THE GUM-GATHERER

There overtook me and drew me in
To his down-hill, early-morning stride,
And set me five miles on my road

The Gum-Gatherer

Better than if he had had me ride,
A man with a swinging bag for load
And half the bag wound round his hand.
We talked like barking above the din
Of water we walked along beside.
And for my telling him where I'd been
And where I lived in mountain land
To be coming home the way I was,
He told me a little about himself.
He came from higher up in the pass
Where the grist of the new-beginning brooks
Is blocks split off the mountain mass—
And hopeless grist enough it looks
Ever to grind to soil for grass.
(The way it is will do for moss.)
There he had built his stolen shack.
It had to be a stolen shack
Because of the fears of fire and loss
That trouble the sleep of lumber folk:
Visions of half the world burned black
And the sun shrunken yellow in smoke.
We know who when they come to town
Bring berries under the wagon seat,
Or a basket of eggs between their feet;
What this man brought in a cotton sack
Was gum, the gum of the mountain spruce.
He showed me lumps of the scented stuff
Like uncut jewels, dull and rough.
It comes to market golden brown;
But turns to pink between the teeth.

I told him this is a pleasant life
To set your breast to the bark of trees
That all your days are dim beneath,

And reaching up with a little knife,
To loose the resin and take it down
And bring it to market when you please.

THE LINE-GANG

Here come the line-gang pioneering by.
They throw a forest down less cut than broken.
They plant dead trees for living, and the dead
They string together with a living thread.
They string an instrument against the sky
Wherein words whether beaten out or spoken
Will run as hushed as when they were a thought
But in no hush they string it: they go past
With shouts afar to pull the cable taut,
To hold it hard until they make it fast,
To ease away—they have it. With a laugh,
An oath of towns that set the wild at naught
They bring the telephone and telegraph.

THE VANISHING RED

He is said to have been the last Red Man
In Acton. And the Miller is said to have laughed—
If you like to call such a sound a laugh.
But he gave no one else a laugher's license.
For he turned suddenly grave as if to say,
'Whose business,—if I take it on myself,
Whose business—but why talk round the barn?—
When it's just that I hold with getting a thing done with.'
You can't get back and see it as he saw it.
It's too long a story to go into now.

The Sound of Trees

You'd have to have been there and lived it.
Then you wouldn't have looked on it as just a matter
Of who began it between the two races.

Some guttural exclamation of surprise
The Red Man gave in poking about the mill
Over the great big thumping shuffling millstone
Disgusted the Miller physically as coming
From one who had no right to be heard from.
'Come, John,' he said, 'you want to see the wheel-pit?'

He took him down below a cramping rafter,
And showed him, through a manhole in the floor,
The water in desperate straits like frantic fish,
Salmon and sturgeon, lashing with their tails.
Then he shut down the trap door with a ring in it
That jangled even above the general noise,
And came upstairs alone—and gave that laugh,
And said something to a man with a meal-sack
That the man with the meal-sack didn't catch—then.
Oh, yes, he showed John the wheel-pit all right.

THE SOUND OF TREES

I wonder about the trees.
Why do we wish to bear
Forever the noise of these
More than another noise
So close to our dwelling place?
We suffer them by the day
Till we lose all measure of pace,
And fixity in our joys,
And acquire a listening air.

They are that that talks of going
But never gets away;
And that talks no less for knowing,
As it grows wiser and older,
That now it means to stay.
My feet tug at the floor
And my head sways to my shoulder
Sometimes when I watch trees sway,
From the window or the door.
I shall set forth for somewhere,
I shall make the reckless choice
Some day when they are in voice
And tossing so as to scare
The white clouds over them on.
I shall have less to say,
But I shall be gone.

New Hampshire

NEW HAMPSHIRE

I met a lady from the South who said
(You won't believe she said it, but she said it):
'None of my family ever worked, or had
A thing to sell.' I don't suppose the work
Much matters. You may work for all of me.
I've seen the time I've had to work myself.
The having anything to sell is what
Is the disgrace in man or state or nation.

I met a traveler from Arkansas
Who boasted of his state as beautiful
For diamonds and apples. 'Diamonds
And apples in commercial quantities?'
I asked him, on my guard. 'Oh, yes,' he answered,
Off his. The time was evening in the Pullman.
'I see the porter's made your bed,' I told him.

I met a Californian who would
Talk California—a state so blessed,
He said, in climate, none had ever died there
A natural death, and Vigilance Committees
Had had to organize to stock the graveyards
And vindicate the state's humanity.
'Just the way Stefansson runs on,' I murmured,
'About the British Arctic. That's what comes
Of being in the market with a climate.'

I met a poet from another state,
A zealot full of fluid inspiration,
Who in the name of fluid inspiration,
But in the best style of bad salesmanship,
Angrily tried to make me write a protest
(In verse I think) against the Volstead Act.
He didn't even offer me a drink
Until I asked for one to steady *him*.
This is called having an idea to sell.

It never could have happened in New Hampshire.

The only person really soiled with trade
I ever stumbled on in old New Hampshire
Was someone who had just come back ashamed
From selling things in California.
He'd built a noble mansard roof with balls
On turrets like Constantinople, deep
In woods some ten miles from a railroad station,
As if to put forever out of mind
The hope of being, as we say, received.
I found him standing at the close of day
Inside the threshold of his open barn,
Like a lone actor on a gloomy stage—

And recognized him through the iron gray
In which his face was muffled to the eyes
As an old boyhood friend, and once indeed
A drover with me on the road to Brighton.
His farm was 'grounds,' and not a farm at all;
His house among the local sheds and shanties
Rose like a factor's at a trading station.
And he was rich, and I was still a rascal.
I couldn't keep from asking impolitely,
Where had he been and what had he been doing?
How did he get so? (Rich was understood.)
In dealing in 'old rags' in San Francisco.
Oh, it was terrible as well could be.
We both of us turned over in our graves.

Just specimens is all New Hampshire has,
One each of everything as in a show-case
Which naturally she doesn't care to sell.

She had one President (pronounce him Purse,
And make the most of it for better or worse.
He's your one chance to score against the state).
She had one Daniel Webster. He was all
The Daniel Webster ever was or shall be.
She had the Dartmouth needed to produce him.

I call her old. She has one family
Whose claim is good to being settled here
Before the era of colonization,
And before that of exploration even.
John Smith remarked them as he coasted by
Dangling their legs and fishing off a wharf
At the Isles of Shoals, and satisfied himself
They weren't Red Indians, but veritable

97

Pre-primitives of the white race, dawn people,
Like those who furnished Adam's sons with wives;
However uninnocent they may have been
In being there so early in our history.
They'd been there then a hundred years or more.
Pity he didn't ask what they were up to
At that date with a wharf already built,
And take their name. They've since told me their name—
Today an honored one in Nottingham.
As for what they were up to more than fishing—
Suppose they weren't behaving Puritanly,
The hour had not yet struck for being good,
Mankind had not yet gone on the Sabbatical.
It became an explorer of the deep
Not to explore too deep in others' business.

Did you but know of him, New Hampshire has
One real reformer who would change the world
So it would be accepted by two classes,
Artists the minute they set up as artists,
Before, that is, they are themselves accepted,
And boys the minute they get out of college.
I can't help thinking those are tests to go by.

And she has one I don't know what to call him,
Who comes from Philadelphia every year
With a great flock of chickens of rare breeds
He wants to give the educational
Advantages of growing almost wild
Under the watchful eye of hawk and eagle—
Dorkings because they're spoken of by Chaucer,
Sussex because they're spoken of by Herrick.

She has a touch of gold. New Hampshire gold—
You may have heard of it. I had a farm

Offered me not long since up Berlin way
With a mine on it that was worked for gold;
But not gold in commercial quantities,
Just enough gold to make the engagement rings
And marriage rings of those who owned the farm.
What gold more innocent could one have asked for?
One of my children ranging after rocks
Lately brought home from Andover or Canaan
A specimen of beryl with a trace
Of radium. I know with radium
The trace would have to be the merest trace
To be below the threshold of commercial;
But trust New Hampshire not to have enough
Of radium or anything to sell.

A specimen of everything, I said.
She has one witch—old style. She lives in Colebrook.
(The only other witch I ever met
Was lately at a cut-glass dinner in Boston.
There were four candles and four people present.
The witch was young, and beautiful (new style),
And open-minded. She was free to question
Her gift for reading letters locked in boxes.
Why was it so much greater when the boxes
Were metal than it was when they were wooden?
It made the world seem so mysterious.
The S'ciety for Psychical Research
Was cognizant. Her husband was worth millions.
I think he owned some shares in Harvard College.)

New Hampshire *used* to have at Salem
A company we called the White Corpuscles,
Whose duty was at any hour of night
To rush in sheets and fools' caps where they smelled

New Hampshire

A thing the least bit doubtfully perscented
And give someone the Skipper Ireson's Ride.

One each of everything as in a show-case.
More than enough land for a specimen
You'll say she has, but there there enters in
Something else to protect her from herself.
There quality makes up for quantity.
Not even New Hampshire farms are much for sale.
The farm I made my home on in the mountains
I had to take by force rather than buy.
I caught the owner outdoors by himself
Raking up after winter, and I said,
'I'm going to put you off this farm: I want it.'
'Where are you going to put me? In the road?'
'I'm going to put you on the farm next to it.'
'Why won't the farm next to it do for you?'
'I like this better.' It was really better.

Apples? New Hampshire has them, but unsprayed,
With no suspicion in stem-end or blossom-end
Of vitriol or arsenate of lead,
And so not good for anything but cider.
Her unpruned grapes are flung like lariats
Far up the birches out of reach of man.

A state producing precious metals, stones,
And—writing; none of these except perhaps
The precious literature in quantity
Or quality to worry the producer
About disposing of it. Do you know,
Considering the market, there are more
Poems produced than any other thing?
No wonder poets sometimes have to *seem*

So much more business-like than business men.
Their wares are so much harder to get rid of.

She's one of the two best states in the Union.
Vermont's the other. And the two have been
Yoke-fellows in the sap-yoke from of old
In many Marches. And they lie like wedges,
Thick end to thin end and thin end to thick end,
And are a figure of the way the strong
Of mind and strong of arm should fit together,
One thick where one is thin and vice versa.
New Hampshire raises the Connecticut
In a trout hatchery near Canada,
But soon divides the river with Vermont.
Both are delightful states for their absurdly
Small towns—Lost Nation, Bungey, Muddy Boo,
Poplin, Still Corners (so called not because
The place is silent all day long, nor yet
Because it boasts a whisky still—because
It set out once to be a city and still
Is only corners, cross-roads in a wood).
And I remember one whose name appeared
Between the pictures on a movie screen
Election night once in Franconia,
When everything had gone Republican
And Democrats were sore in need of comfort:
Easton goes Democratic, Wilson 4
Hughes 2. And everybody to the saddest
Laughed the loud laugh, the big laugh at the little.
New York (five million) laughs at Manchester,
Manchester (sixty or seventy thousand) laughs
At Littleton (four thousand), Littleton
Laughs at Franconia (seven hundred), and
Franconia laughs, I fear,—did laugh that night—

New Hampshire

At Easton. What has Easton left to laugh at,
And like the actress exclaim, 'Oh, my God' at?
There's Bungey; and for Bungey there are towns,
Whole townships named but without population.

Anything I can say about New Hampshire
Will serve almost as well about Vermont,
Excepting that they differ in their mountains.
The Vermont mountains stretch extended straight;
New Hampshire mountains curl up in a coil.

I had been coming to New Hampshire mountains.
And here I am and what am I to say?
Here first my theme becomes embarrassing.
Emerson said, 'The God who made New Hampshire
Taunted the lofty land with little men.'
Another Massachusetts poet said,
'I go no more to summer in New Hampshire.
I've given up my summer place in Dublin.'
But when I asked to know what ailed New Hampshire,
She said she couldn't stand the people in it,
The little men (it's Massachusetts speaking).
And when I asked to know what ailed the people,
She said, 'Go read your own books and find out.'
I may as well confess myself the author
Of several books against the world in general.
To take them as against a special state
Or even nation's to restrict my meaning.
I'm what is called a sensibilitist,
Or otherwise an environmentalist.
I refuse to adapt myself a mite
To any change from hot to cold, from wet
To dry, from poor to rich, or back again.
I make a virtue of my suffering

From nearly everything that goes on round me.
In other words, I know wherever I am,
Being the creature of literature I am,
I shall not lack for pain to keep me awake.
Kit Marlowe taught me how to say my prayers:
'Why, this is Hell, nor am I out of it.'
Samoa, Russia, Ireland, I complain of,
No less than England, France, and Italy.
Because I wrote my novels in New Hampshire
Is no proof that I aimed them at New Hampshire.

When I left Massachusetts years ago
Between two days, the reason why I sought
New Hampshire, not Connecticut,
Rhode Island, New York, or Vermont was this:
Where I was living then, New Hampshire offered
The nearest boundary to escape across.
I hadn't an illusion in my hand-bag
About the people being better there
Than those I left behind. I thought they weren't.
I thought they couldn't be. And yet they were.
I'd sure had no such friends in Massachusetts
As Hall of Windham, Gay of Atkinson,
Bartlett of Raymond (now of Colorado),
Harris of Derry, and Lynch of Bethlehem.

The glorious bards of Massachusetts seem
To want to make New Hampshire people over.
They taunt the lofty land with little men.
I don't know what to say about the people.
For art's sake one could almost wish them worse
Rather than better. How are we to write
The Russian novel in America
As long as life goes so unterribly?
There is the pinch from which our only outcry

New Hampshire

In literature to date is heard to come.
We get what little misery we can
Out of not having cause for misery.
It makes the guild of novel writers sick
To be expected to be Dostoievskis
On nothing worse than too much luck and comfort.
This is not sorrow, though; it's just the vapors,
And recognized as such in Russia itself
Under the new régime, and so forbidden.
If well it is with Russia, then feel free
To say so or be stood against the wall
And shot. It's Pollyanna now or death.
This, then, is the new freedom we hear tell of;
And very sensible. No state can build
A literature that shall at once be sound
And sad on a foundation of well-being.

To show the level of intelligence
Among us: it was just a Warren farmer
Whose horse had pulled him short up in the road
By me, a stranger. This is what he said,
From nothing but embarrassment and want
Of anything more sociable to say:
'You hear those hound-dogs sing on Moosilauke?
Well they remind me of the hue and cry
We've heard against the Mid-Victorians
And never rightly understood till Bryan
Retired from politics and joined the chorus.
The matter with the Mid-Victorians
Seems to have been a man named John L. Darwin.'
'Go 'long,' I said to him, he to his horse.

I knew a man who failing as a farmer
Burned down his farmhouse for the fire insurance,
And spent the proceeds on a telescope

New Hampshire

To satisfy a life-long curiosity
About our place among the infinities.
And how was that for other-worldliness?

If I must choose which I would elevate—
The people or the already lofty mountains,
I'd elevate the already lofty mountains.
The only fault I find with old New Hampshire
Is that her mountains aren't quite high enough.
I was not always so; I've come to be so.
How, to my sorrow, how have I attained
A height from which to look down critical
On mountains? What has given me assurance
To say what height becomes New Hampshire mountains,
Or any mountains? Can it be some strength
I feel as of an earthquake in my back
To heave them higher to the morning star?
Can it be foreign travel in the Alps?
Or having seen and credited a moment
The solid molding of vast peaks of cloud
Behind the pitiful reality
Of Lincoln, Lafayette, and Liberty?
Or some such sense as says how high shall jet
The fountain in proportion to the basin?
No, none of these has raised me to my throne
Of intellectual dissatisfaction,
But the sad accident of having seen
Our actual mountains given in a map
Of early times as twice the height they are—
Ten thousand feet instead of only five—
Which shows how sad an accident may be.
Five thousand is no longer high enough.
Whereas I never had a good idea
About improving people in the world,

New Hampshire

Here I am over-fertile in suggestion,
And cannot rest from planning day or night
How high I'd thrust the peaks in summer snow
To tap the upper sky and draw a flow
Of frosty night air on the vale below
Down from the stars to freeze the dew as starry.

The more the sensibilitist I am
The more I seem to want my mountains wild;
The way the wiry gang-boss liked the log-jam.
After he'd picked the lock and got it started,
He dodged a log that lifted like an arm
Against the sky to break his back for him,
Then came in dancing, skipping, with his life
Across the roar and chaos, and the words
We saw him say along the zigzag journey
Were doubtless as the words we heard him say
On coming nearer: 'Wasn't she an *i*-deal
Son-of-a-bitch? You bet she was an *i*-deal.'

For all her mountains fall a little short,
Her people not quite short enough for Art,
She's still New Hampshire, a most restful state.

Lately in converse with a New York alec
About the new school of the pseudo-phallic,
I found myself in a close corner where
I had to make an almost funny choice.
'Choose you which you will be—a prude, or puke,
Mewling and puking in the public arms.'
'Me for the hills where I don't have to choose.'
'But if you had to choose, which would you be?'
I wouldn't be a prude afraid of nature.
I know a man who took a double ax

And went alone against a grove of trees;
But his heart failing him, he dropped the ax
And ran for shelter quoting Matthew Arnold:
'Nature is cruel, man is sick of blood;
There's been enough shed without shedding mine.
Remember Birnam Wood! The wood's in flux!'
He had a special terror of the flux
That showed itself in dendrophobia.
The only decent tree had been to mill
And educated into boards, he said.
He knew too well for any earthly use
The line where man leaves off and nature starts,
And never over-stepped it save in dreams.
He stood on the safe side of the line talking;
Which is sheer Matthew Arnoldism,
The cult of one who owned himself 'a foiled,
Circuitous wanderer,' and 'took dejectedly
His seat upon the intellectual throne.'
Agreed in frowning on these improvised
Altars the woods are full of nowadays,
Again as in the days when Ahaz sinned
By worship under green trees in the open.
Scarcely a mile but that I come on one,
A black-cheeked stone and stick of rain-washed charcoal
Even to say the groves were God's first temples
Comes too near to Ahaz' sin for safety.
Nothing not built with hands of course is sacred.
But here is not a question of what's sacred;
Rather of what to face or run away from.
I'd hate to be a runaway from nature.
And neither would I choose to be a puke
Who cares not what he does in company,
And, when he can't do anything, falls back
On words, and tries his worst to make words speak

Louder than actions, and sometimes achieves it.
It seems a narrow choice the age insists on.
How about being a good Greek, for instance?
That course, they tell me, isn't offered this year.
'Come, but this isn't choosing—puke or prude?'
Well, if I have to choose one or the other,
I choose to be a plain New Hampshire farmer
With an income in cash of say a thousand
(From say a publisher in New York City).
It's restful to arrive at a decision,
And restful just to think about New Hampshire.
At present I am living in Vermont.

A STAR IN A STONE-BOAT

for Lincoln MacVeagh

Never tell me that not one star of all
That slip from heaven at night and softly fall
Has been picked up with stones to build a wall.

Some laborer found one faded and stone cold,
And saving that its weight suggested gold,
And tugged it from his first too certain hold,

He noticed nothing in it to remark.
He was not used to handling stars thrown dark
And lifeless from an interrupted arc.

He did not recognize in that smooth coal
The one thing palpable beside the soul
To penetrate the air in which we roll.

He did not see how like a flying thing
It brooded ant-eggs, and had one large wing,
One not so large for flying in a ring,

A Star in a Stone-Boat

And a long Bird of Paradise's tail,
(Though these when not in use to fly and trail
It drew back in its body like a snail);

Nor know that he might move it from the spot,
The harm was done; from having been star-shot
The very nature of the soil was hot

And burning to yield flowers instead of grain,
Flowers fanned and not put out by all the rain
Poured on them by his prayers prayed in vain.

He moved it roughly with an iron bar,
He loaded an old stone-boat with the star
And not, as you might think, a flying car,

Such as even poets would admit perforce
More practical than Pegasus the horse
If it could put a star back in its course.

He dragged it through the plowed ground at a pace
But faintly reminiscent of the race
Of jostling rock in interstellar space.

It went for building stone, and I, as though
Commanded in a dream, forever go
To right the wrong that this should have been so.

Yet ask where else it could have gone as well,
I do not know—I cannot stop to tell:
He might have left it lying where it fell.

From following walls I never lift my eye
Except at night to places in the sky
Where showers of charted meteors let fly.

Some may know what they seek in school and church,
And why they seek it there; for what I search
I must go measuring stone walls, perch on perch;

Sure that though not a star of death and birth,
So not to be compared, perhaps, in worth
To such resorts of life as Mars and Earth,

Though not, I say, a star of death and sin
It yet has poles, and only needs a spin
To show its worldly nature and begin

To chafe and shuffle in my calloused palm
And run off in strange tangents with my arm
As fish do with the line in first alarm.

Such as it is, it promises the prize
Of the one world complete in any size
That I am like to compass, fool or wise.

THE CENSUS-TAKER

I came an errand one cloud-blowing evening
To a slab-built, black-paper-covered house
Of one room and one window and one door,
The only dwelling in a waste cut over
A hundred square miles round it in the mountains:
And that not dwelt in now by men or women.
(It never had been dwelt in, though, by women,
So what is this I make a sorrow of?)
I came as census-taker to the waste
To count the people in it and found none,
None in the hundred miles, none in the house,
Where I came last with some hope, but not much
After hours' overlooking from the cliffs

An emptiness flayed to the very stone.
I found no people that dared show themselves,
None not in hiding from the outward eye.
The time was autumn, but how anyone
Could tell the time of year when every tree
That could have dropped a leaf was down itself
And nothing but the stump of it was left
Now bringing out its rings in sugar of pitch;
And every tree up stood a rotting trunk
Without a single leaf to spend on autumn,
Or branch to whistle after what was spent.
Perhaps the wind the more without the help
Of breathing trees said something of the time
Of year or day the way it swung a door
Forever off the latch, as if rude men
Passed in and slammed it shut each one behind him
For the next one to open for himself.
I counted nine I had no right to count
(But this was dreamy unofficial counting)
Before I made the tenth across the threshold.
Where was my supper? Where was anyone's?
No lamp was lit. Nothing was on the table.
The stove was cold—the stove was off the chimney—
And down by one side where it lacked a leg.
The people that had loudly passed the door
Were people to the ear but not the eye.
They were not on the table with their elbows.
They were not sleeping in the shelves of bunks.
I saw no men there and no bones of men there.
I armed myself against such bones as might be
With the pitch-blackened stub of an ax-handle
I picked up off the straw-dust covered floor.
Not bones, but the ill-fitted window rattled.
The door was still because I held it shut

While I thought what to do that could be done—
About the house—about the people not there.
This house in one year fallen to decay
Filled me with no less sorrow than the houses
Fallen to ruin in ten thousand years
Where Asia wedges Africa from Europe.
Nothing was left to do that I could see
Unless to find that there was no one there
And declare to the cliffs too far for echo,
'The place is desert and let whoso lurks
In silence, if in this he is aggrieved,
Break silence now or be forever silent.
Let him say why it should not be declared so.'
The melancholy of having to count souls
Where they grow fewer and fewer every year
Is extreme where they shrink to none at all.
It must be I want life to go on living.

THE STAR-SPLITTER

'You know Orion always comes up sideways.
Throwing a leg up over our fence of mountains,
And rising on his hands, he looks in on me
Busy outdoors by lantern-light with something
I should have done by daylight, and indeed,
After the ground is frozen, I should have done
Before it froze, and a gust flings a handful
Of waste leaves at my smoky lantern chimney
To make fun of my way of doing things,
Or else fun of Orion's having caught me.
Has a man, I should like to ask, no rights
These forces are obliged to pay respect to?'
So Brad McLaughlin mingled reckless talk
Of heavenly stars with hugger-mugger farming,

Till having failed at hugger-mugger farming,
He burned his house down for the fire insurance
And spent the proceeds on a telescope
To satisfy a life-long curiosity
About our place among the infinities.

'What do you want with one of those blame things?'
I asked him well beforehand. 'Don't you get one!'
'Don't call it blamed; there isn't anything
More blameless in the sense of being less
A weapon in our human fight,' he said.
'I'll have one if I sell my farm to buy it.'
There where he moved the rocks to plow the ground
And plowed between the rocks he couldn't move,
Few farms changed hands; so rather than spend years
Trying to sell his farm and then not selling,
He burned his house down for the fire insurance
And bought the telescope with what it came to.
He had been heard to say by several:
'The best thing that we're put here for's to see;
The strongest thing that's given us to see with's
A telescope. Someone in every town
Seems to me owes it to the town to keep one.
In Littleton it may as well be me.'
After such loose talk it was no surprise
When he did what he did and burned his house down.

Mean laughter went about the town that day
To let him know we weren't the least imposed on,
And he could wait—we'd see to him tomorrow.
But the first thing next morning we reflected
If one by one we counted people out
For the least sin, it wouldn't take us long
To get so we had no one left to live with.
For to be social is to be forgiving.

Our thief, the one who does our stealing from us,
We don't cut off from coming to church suppers,
But what we miss we go to him and ask for.
He promptly gives it back, that is if still
Uneaten, unworn out, or undisposed of.
It wouldn't do to be too hard on Brad
About his telescope. Beyond the age
Of being given one for Christmas gift,
He had to take the best way he knew how
To find himself in one. Well, all we said was
He took a strange thing to be roguish over.
Some sympathy was wasted on the house,
A good old-timer dating back along;
But a house isn't sentient; the house
Didn't feel anything. And if it did,
Why not regard it as a sacrifice,
And an old-fashioned sacrifice by fire,
Instead of a new-fashioned one at auction?

Out of a house and so out of a farm
At one stroke (of a match), Brad had to turn
To earn a living on the Concord railroad,
As under-ticket-agent at a station
Where his job, when he wasn't selling tickets,
Was setting out up track and down, not plants
As on a farm, but planets, evening stars
That varied in their hue from red to green.

He got a good glass for six hundred dollars.
His new job gave him leisure for star-gazing.
Often he bid me come and have a look
Up the brass barrel, velvet black inside,
At a star quaking in the other end.
I recollect a night of broken clouds
And underfoot snow melted down to ice,

And melting further in the wind to mud.
Bradford and I had out the telescope.
We spread our two legs as we spread its three,
Pointed our thoughts the way we pointed it,
And standing at our leisure till the day broke,
Said some of the best things we ever said.
That telescope was christened the Star-splitter,
Because it didn't do a thing but split
A star in two or three the way you split
A globule of quicksilver in your hand
With one stroke of your finger in the middle.
It's a star-splitter if there ever was one
And ought to do some good if splitting stars
'Sa thing to be compared with splitting wood.

We've looked and looked, but after all where are we?
Do we know any better where we are,
And how it stands between the night tonight
And a man with a smoky lantern chimney?
How different from the way it ever stood?

THE GRINDSTONE

Having a wheel and four legs of its own
Has never availed the cumbersome grindstone
To get it anywhere that I can see.
These hands have helped it go, and even race;
Not all the motion, though, they ever lent,
Not all the miles it may have thought it went,
Have got it one step from the starting place.
It stands beside the same old apple tree.
The shadow of the apple tree is thin
Upon it now, its feet are fast in snow.
All other farm machinery's gone in,

And some of it on no more legs and wheel
Than the grindstone can boast to stand or go.
(I'm thinking chiefly of the wheelbarrow.)
For months it hasn't known the taste of steel,
Washed down with rusty water in a tin.
But standing outdoors hungry, in the cold,
Except in towns at night, is not a sin.
And, anyway, its standing in the yard
Under a ruinous live apple tree
Has nothing any more to do with me,
Except that I remember how of old
One summer day, all day I drove it hard,
And someone mounted on it rode it hard,
And he and I between us ground a blade.

I gave it the preliminary spin,
And poured on water (tears it might have been),
And when it almost gaily jumped and flowed,
A Father-Time-like man got on and rode,
Armed with a scythe and spectacles that glowed.
He turned on will-power to increase the load
And slow me down—and I abruptly slowed,
Like coming to a sudden railroad station.
I changed from hand to hand in desperation.
I wondered what machine of ages gone
This represented an improvement on.
For all I knew it may have sharpened spears
And arrowheads itself. Much use for years
Had gradually worn it an oblate
Spheroid that kicked and struggled in its gait,
Appearing to return me hate for hate;
(But I forgive it now as easily
As any other boyhood enemy
Whose pride has failed to get him anywhere).

The Grindstone

I wondered who it was the man thought ground—
The one who held the wheel back or the one
Who gave his life to keep it going round?
I wondered if he really thought it fair
For him to have the say when we were done.
Such were the bitter thoughts to which I turned.

Not for myself was I so much concerned.
Oh no!—although, of course, I could have found
A better way to pass the afternoon
Than grinding discord out of a grindstone,
And beating insects at their gritty tune.
Nor was I for the man so much concerned.
Once when the grindstone almost jumped its bearing
It looked as if he might be badly thrown
And wounded on his blade. So far from caring,
I laughed inside, and only cranked the faster,
(It ran as if it wasn't greased but glued);
I'd welcome any moderate disaster
That might be calculated to postpone
What evidently nothing could conclude.
The thing that made me more and more afraid
Was that we'd ground it sharp and hadn't known.
And now were only wasting precious blade.
And when he raised it dripping once and tried
The creepy edge of it with wary touch,
And viewed it over his glasses funny-eyed,
Only disinterestedly to decide
It needed a turn more, I could have cried
Wasn't there danger of a turn too much?
Mightn't we make it worse instead of better?
I was for leaving something to the whetter.
What if it wasn't all it should be? I'd
Be satisfied if he'd be satisfied.

PAUL'S WIFE

To drive Paul out of any lumber camp
All that was needed was to say to him,
'How is the wife, Paul?'—and he'd disappear.
Some said it was because he had no wife,
And hated to be twitted on the subject;
Others because he'd come within a day
Or so of having one, and then been jilted;
Others because he'd had one once, a good one,
Who'd run away with someone else and left him;
And others still because he had one now
He only had to be reminded of,—
He was all duty to her in a minute:
He had to run right off to look her up,
As if to say, 'That's so, how is my wife?
I hope she isn't getting into mischief.'
No one was anxious to get rid of Paul.
He'd been the hero of the mountain camps
Ever since, just to show them, he had slipped
The bark of a whole tamarack off whole,
As clean as boys do off a willow twig
To make a willow whistle on a Sunday
In April by subsiding meadow brooks.
They seemed to ask him just to see him go,
'How is the wife, Paul?' and he always went.
He never stopped to murder anyone
Who asked the question. He just disappeared—
Nobody knew in what direction,
Although it wasn't usually long
Before they heard of him in some new camp,
The same Paul at the same old feats of logging.
The question everywhere was why should Paul

Paul's Wife

Object to being asked a civil question—
A man you could say almost anything to
Short of a fighting word. You have the answers.
And there was one more not so fair to Paul:
That Paul had married a wife not his equal.
Paul was ashamed of her. To match a hero,
She would have had to be a heroine;
Instead of which she was some half-breed squaw.
But if the story Murphy told was true,
She wasn't anything to be ashamed of.

You know Paul could do wonders. Everyone's
Heard how he thrashed the horses on a load
That wouldn't budge until they simply stretched
Their rawhide harness from the load to camp.
Paul told the boss the load would be all right,
'The sun will bring your load in'—and it did—
By shrinking the rawhide to natural length.
That's what is called a stretcher. But I guess
The one about his jumping so's to land
With both his feet at once against the ceiling,
And then land safely right side up again,
Back on the floor, is fact or pretty near fact.
Well, this is such a yarn. Paul sawed his wife
Out of a white-pine log. Murphy was there,
And, as you might say, saw the lady born.
Paul worked at anything in lumbering.
He'd been hard at it taking boards away
For—I forget—the last ambitious sawyer
To want to find out if he couldn't pile
The lumber on Paul till Paul begged for mercy.
They'd sliced the first slab off a big butt log,
And the sawyer had slammed the carriage back
To slam end on again against the saw teeth.

To judge them by the way they caught themselves
When they saw what had happened to the log,
They must have had a guilty expectation
Something was going to go with their slambanging.
Something had left a broad black streak of grease
On the new wood the whole length of the log
Except, perhaps, a foot at either end.
But when Paul put his finger in the grease,
It wasn't grease at all, but a long slot.
The log was hollow. They were sawing pine.
'First time I ever saw a hollow pine.
That comes of having Paul around the place.
Take it to hell for me,' the sawyer said.
Everyone had to have a look at it,
And tell Paul what he ought to do about it.
(They treated it as his.) 'You take a jack-knife,
And spread the opening, and you've got a dug-out
All dug to go a-fishing in.' To Paul
The hollow looked too sound and clean and empty
Ever to have housed birds or beasts or bees.
There was no entrance for them to get in by.
It looked to him like some new kind of hollow
He thought he'd *better* take his jack-knife to.
So after work that evening he came back
And let enough light into it by cutting
To see if it was empty. He made out in there
A slender length of pith, or was it pith?
It might have been the skin a snake had cast
And left stood up on end inside the tree
The hundred years the tree must have been growing.
More cutting and he had this in both hands,
And, looking from it to the pond nearby,
Paul wondered how it would respond to water.
Not a breeze stirred, but just the breath of air

Paul's Wife

He made in walking slowly to the beach
Blew it once off his hands and almost broke it.
He laid it at the edge where it could drink.
At the first drink it rustled and grew limp.
At the next drink it grew invisible.
Paul dragged the shallows for it with his fingers,
And thought it must have melted. It was gone.
And then beyond the open water, dim with midges,
Where the log drive lay pressed against the boom,
It slowly rose a person, rose a girl,
Her wet hair heavy on her like a helmet,
Who, leaning on a log looked back at Paul.
And that made Paul in turn look back
To see if it was anyone behind him
That she was looking at instead of him.
Murphy had been there watching all the time,
But from a shed where neither of them could see him.
There was a moment of suspense in birth
When the girl seemed too water-logged to live,
Before she caught her first breath with a gasp
And laughed. Then she climbed slowly to her feet,
And walked off talking to herself or Paul
Across the logs like backs of alligators,
Paul taking after her around the pond.

Next evening Murphy and some other fellows
Got drunk, and tracked the pair up Catamount,
From the bare top of which there is a view
To other hills across a kettle valley.
And there, well after dark, let Murphy tell it,
They saw Paul and his creature keeping house.
It was the only glimpse that anyone
Has had of Paul and her since Murphy saw them
Falling in love across the twilight mill-pond.

More than a mile across the wilderness
They sat together halfway up a cliff
In a small niche let into it, the girl
Brightly, as if a star played on the place,
Paul darkly, like her shadow. All the light
Was from the girl herself, though, not from a star,
As was apparent from what happened next.
All those great ruffians put their throats together,
And let out a loud yell, and threw a bottle,
As a brute tribute of respect to beauty.
Of course the bottle fell short by a mile,
But the shout reached the girl and put her light out.
She went out like a firefly, and that was all.

So there were witnesses that Paul was married,
And not to anyone to be ashamed of.
Everyone had been wrong in judging Paul.
Murphy told me Paul put on all those airs
About his wife to keep her to himself.
Paul was what's called a terrible possessor.
Owning a wife with him meant owning her.
She wasn't anybody else's business,
Either to praise her, or so much as name her,
And he'd thank people not to think of her.
Murphy's idea was that a man like Paul
Wouldn't be spoken to about a wife
In any way the world knew how to speak.

WILD GRAPES

What tree may not the fig be gathered from?
The grape may not be gathered from the birch?

Wild Grapes

It's all you know the grape, or know the birch.
As a girl gathered from the birch myself
Equally with my weight in grapes, one autumn,
I ought to know what tree the grape is fruit of.
I was born, I suppose, like anyone,
And grew to be a little boyish girl
My brother could not always leave at home.
But that beginning was wiped out in fear
The day I swung suspended with the grapes,
And was come after like Eurydice
And brought down safely from the upper regions;
And the life I live now's an extra life
I can waste as I please on whom I please.
So if you see me celebrate two birthdays,
And give myself out as two different ages,
One of them five years younger than I look—

One day my brother led me to a glade
Where a white birch he knew of stood alone,
Wearing a thin head-dress of pointed leaves,
And heavy on her heavy hair behind,
Against her neck, an ornament of grapes.
Grapes, I knew grapes from having seen them last year.
One bunch of them, and there began to be
Bunches all round me growing in white birches,
The way they grew round Leif the Lucky's German;
Mostly as much beyond my lifted hands, though,
As the moon used to seem when I was younger,
And only freely to be had for climbing.
My brother did the climbing; and at first
Threw me down grapes to miss and scatter
And have to hunt for in sweet fern and hardhack;
Which gave him some time to himself to eat,
But not so much, perhaps, as a boy needed.

So then, to make me wholly self-supporting,
He climbed still higher and bent the tree to earth
And put it in my hands to pick my own grapes.
'Here, take a tree-top. I'll get down another.
Hold on with all your might when I let go.'
I said I had the tree. It wasn't true.
The opposite was true. The tree had me.
The minute it was left with me alone
It caught me up as if I were the fish
And it the fishpole. So I was translated
To loud cries from my brother of 'Let go!
Don't you know anything, you girl? Let go!'
But I, with something of the baby grip
Acquired ancestrally in just such trees
When wilder mothers than our wildest now
Hung babies out on branches by the hands
To dry or wash or tan, I don't know which,
(You'll have to ask an evolutionist)—
I held on uncomplainingly for life.
My brother tried to make me laugh to help me.
'What are you doing up there in those grapes?
Don't be afraid. A few of them won't hurt you.
I mean, they won't pick you if you don't them.'
Much danger of my picking anything!
By that time I was pretty well reduced
To a philosophy of hang-and-let-hang.
'Now you know how it feels,' my brother said,
'To be a bunch of fox-grapes, as they call them,
That when it thinks it has escaped the fox
By growing where it shouldn't—on a birch,
Where a fox wouldn't think to look for it—
And if he looked and found it, couldn't reach it—
Just then come you and I to gather it.
Only you have the advantage of the grapes

In one way: you have one more stem to cling by,
And promise more resistance to the picker.'

One by one I lost off my hat and shoes,
And still I clung. I let my head fall back,
And shut my eyes against the sun, my ears
Against my brother's nonsense; 'Drop,' he said,
'I'll catch you in my arms. It isn't far.'
(Stated in lengths of him it might not be.)
'Drop or I'll shake the tree and shake you down.'
Grim silence on my part as I sank lower,
My small wrists stretching till they showed the banjo strings.
'Why, if she isn't serious about it!
Hold tight awhile till I think what to do.
I'll bend the tree down and let you down by it.'
I don't know much about the letting down;
But once I felt ground with my stocking feet
And the world came revolving back to me,
I know I looked long at my curled-up fingers,
Before I straightened them and brushed the bark off.
My brother said: 'Don't you weigh anything?
Try to weigh something next time, so you won't
Be run off with by birch trees into space.'

It wasn't my not weighing anything
So much as my not knowing anything—
My brother had been nearer right before.
I had not taken the first step in knowledge;
I had not learned to let go with the hands,
As still I have not learned to with the heart,
And have no wish to with the heart—nor need,
That I can see. The mind—is not the heart.
I may yet live, as I know others live,
To wish in vain to let go with the mind—

Of cares, at night, to sleep; but nothing tells me
'That I need learn to let go with the heart.

TWO WITCHES

I

THE WITCH OF COÖS

I stayed the night for shelter at a farm
Behind the mountain, with a mother and son,
Two old-believers. They did all the talking.

MOTHER. Folks think a witch who has familiar spirits
She could call up to pass a winter evening,
But won't, should be burned at the stake or something.
Summoning spirits isn't 'Button, button,
Who's got the button,' I would have them know.

SON. Mother can make a common table rear
And kick with two legs like an army mule.

MOTHER. And when I've done it, what good have I done?
Rather than tip a table for you, let me
Tell you what Ralle the Sioux Control once told me.
He said the dead had souls, but when I asked him
How could that be—I thought the dead were souls,
He broke my trance. Don't that make you suspicious
That there's something the dead are keeping back?
Yes, there's something the dead are keeping back.

SON. You wouldn't want to tell him what we have
Up attic, mother?

MOTHER. Bones—a skeleton.

son. But the headboard of mother's bed is pushed
Against the attic door: the door is nailed.
It's harmless. Mother hears it in the night
Halting perplexed behind the barrier
Of door and headboard. Where it wants to get
Is back into the cellar where it came from.

mother. We'll never let them, will we, son! We'll never!

son. It left the cellar forty years ago
And carried itself like a pile of dishes
Up one flight from the cellar to the kitchen,
Another from the kitchen to the bedroom,
Another from the bedroom to the attic,
Right past both father and mother, and neither stopped it.
Father had gone upstairs; mother was downstairs.
I was a baby: I don't know where I was.

mother. The only fault my husband found with me—
I went to sleep before I went to bed,
Especially in winter when the bed
Might just as well be ice and the clothes snow.
The night the bones came up the cellar-stairs
Toffile had gone to bed alone and left me,
But left an open door to cool the room off
So as to sort of turn me out of it.
I was just coming to myself enough
To wonder where the cold was coming from,
When I heard Toffile upstairs in the bedroom
And thought I heard him downstairs in the cellar.
The board we had laid down to walk dry-shod on
When there was water in the cellar in spring
Struck the hard cellar bottom. And then someone
Began the stairs, two footsteps for each step,

127

The way a man with one leg and a crutch,
Or a little child, comes up. It wasn't Toffile:
It wasn't anyone who could be there.
The bulkhead double-doors were double-locked
And swollen tight and buried under snow.
The cellar windows were banked up with sawdust
And swollen tight and buried under snow.
It was the bones. I knew them—and good reason.
My first impulse was to get to the knob
And hold the door. But the bones didn't try
The door; they halted helpless on the landing,
Waiting for things to happen in their favor.
The faintest restless rustling ran all through them.
I never could have done the thing I did
If the wish hadn't been too strong in me
To see how they were mounted for this walk.
I had a vision of them put together
Not like a man, but like a chandelier.
So suddenly I flung the door wide on him.
A moment he stood balancing with emotion,
And all but lost himself. (A tongue of fire
Flashed out and licked along his upper teeth.
Smoke rolled inside the sockets of his eyes.)
Then he came at me with one hand outstretched,
The way he did in life once; but this time
I struck the hand off brittle on the floor,
And fell back from him on the floor myself.
The finger-pieces slid in all directions.
(Where did I see one of those pieces lately?
Hand me my button-box—it must be there.)
I sat up on the floor and shouted, 'Toffile,
It's coming up to you.' It had its choice
Of the door to the cellar or the hall.
It took the hall door for the novelty,

And set off briskly for so slow a thing,
Still going every which way in the joints, though,
So that it looked like lightning or a scribble,
From the slap I had just now given its hand.
I listened till it almost climbed the stairs
From the hall to the only finished bedroom,
Before I got up to do anything;
Then ran and shouted, 'Shut the bedroom door,
Toffile, for my sake!' 'Company?' he said,
'Don't make me get up; I'm too warm in bed.'
So lying forward weakly on the handrail
I pushed myself upstairs, and in the light
(The kitchen had been dark) I had to own
I could see nothing. 'Toffile, I don't see it.
It's with us in the room though. It's the bones.'
'What bones?' 'The cellar bones—out of the grave.'
That made him throw his bare legs out of bed
And sit up by me and take hold of me.
I wanted to put out the light and see
If I could see it, or else mow the room,
With our arms at the level of our knees,
And bring the chalk-pile down. 'I'll tell you what—
It's looking for another door to try.
The uncommonly deep snow has made him think
Of his old song, *The Wild Colonial Boy*,
He always used to sing along the tote road.
He's after an open door to get outdoors.
Let's trap him with an open door up attic.'
Toffile agreed to that, and sure enough,
Almost the moment he was given an opening,
The steps began to climb the attic stairs.
I heard them. Toffile didn't seem to hear them.
'Quick!' I slammed to the door and held the knob.
'Toffile, get nails.' I made him nail the door shut

And push the headboard of the bed against it.
Then we asked was there anything
Up attic that we'd ever want again.
The attic was less to us than the cellar.
If the bones liked the attic, let them have it.
Let them stay in the attic. When they sometimes
Come down the stairs at night and stand perplexed
Behind the door and headboard of the bed,
Brushing their chalky skull with chalky fingers,
With sounds like the dry rattling of a shutter,
That's what I sit up in the dark to say—
To no one any more since Toffile died.
Let them stay in the attic since they went there.
I promised Toffile to be cruel to them
For helping them be cruel once to him.

SON. We think they had a grave down in the cellar.

MOTHER. We know they had a grave down in the cellar.

SON. We never could find out whose bones they were.

MOTHER. Yes, we could too, son. Tell the truth for once.
They were a man's his father killed for me.
I mean a man he killed instead of me.
The least I could do was to help dig their grave.
We were about it one night in the cellar.
Son knows the story: but 'twas not for him
To tell the truth, suppose the time had come.
Son looks surprised to see me end a lie
We'd kept all these years between ourselves
So as to have it ready for outsiders.
But tonight I don't care enough to lie—
I don't remember why I ever cared.
Toffile, if he were here, I don't believe
Could tell you why he ever cared himself. . . .

She hadn't found the finger-bone she wanted
Among the buttons poured out in her lap.
I verified the name next morning: Toffile.
The rural letter box said Toffile Lajway.

II

THE PAUPER WITCH OF GRAFTON

Now that they've got it settled whose I be,
I'm going to tell them something they won't like:
They've got it settled wrong, and I can prove it.
Flattered I must be to have two towns fighting
To make a present of me to each other.
They don't dispose me, either one of them,
To spare them any trouble. Double trouble's
Always the witch's motto anyway.
I'll double theirs for both of them—you watch me.
They'll find they've got the whole thing to do over,
That is, if facts is what they want to go by.
They set a lot (now don't they?) by a record
Of Arthur Amy's having once been up
For Hog Reeve in March Meeting here in Warren.
I could have told them any time this twelvemonth
The Arthur Amy I was married to
Couldn't have been the one they say was up
In Warren at March Meeting for the reason
He wa'n't but fifteen at the time they say.
The Arthur Amy I was married to
Voted the only times he ever voted,
Which wasn't many, in the town of Wentworth.
One of the times was when 'twas in the warrant
To see if the town wanted to take over

The tote road to our clearing where we lived.
I'll tell you who'd remember—Heman Lapish.
Their Arthur Amy was the father of mine.
So now they've dragged it through the law courts once
I guess they'd better drag it through again.
Wentworth and Warren's both good towns to live in,
Only I happen to prefer to live
In Wentworth from now on; and when all's said,
Right's right, and the temptation to do right
When I can hurt someone by doing it
Has always been too much for me, it has.
I know of some folks that'd be set up
At having in their town a noted witch:
But most would have to think of the expense
That even I would be. They ought to know
That as a witch I'd often milk a bat
And that'd be enough to last for days.
It'd make my position stronger, think,
If I was to consent to give some sign
To make it surer that I was a witch?
It wa'n't no sign, I s'pose, when Mallice Huse
Said that I took him out in his old age
And rode all over everything on him
Until I'd had him worn to skin and bones,
And if I'd left him hitched unblanketed
In front of one Town Hall, I'd left him hitched
In front of every one in Grafton County.
Some cried shame on me not to blanket him,
The poor old man. It would have been all right
If someone hadn't said to gnaw the posts
He stood beside and leave his trade mark on them,
So they could recognize them. Not a post
That they could hear tell of was scarified.
They made him keep on gnawing till he whined.

Then that same smarty someone said to look—
He'd bet Huse was a cribber and had gnawed
The crib he slept in—and as sure's you're born
They found he'd gnawed the four posts of his bed,
All four of them to splinters. What did that prove?
Not that he hadn't gnawed the hitching posts
He said he had besides. Because a horse
Gnaws in the stable ain't no proof to me
He don't gnaw trees and posts and fences too.
But everybody took it for a proof.
I was a strapping girl of twenty then.
The smarty someone who spoiled everything
Was Arthur Amy. You know who he was.
That was the way he started courting me.
He never said much after we were married,
But I mistrusted he was none too proud
Of having interfered in the Huse business.
I guess he found he got more out of me
By having me a witch. Or something happened
To turn him round. He got to saying things
To undo what he'd done and make it right,
Like, 'No, she ain't come back from kiting yet.
Last night was one of her nights out. She's kiting.
She thinks when the wind makes a night of it
She might as well herself.' But he liked best
To let on he was plagued to death with me:
If anyone had seen me coming home
Over the ridgepole, 'stride of a broomstick,
As often as he had in the tail of the night,
He guessed they'd know what he had to put up with.
Well, I showed Arthur Amy signs enough
Off from the house as far as we could keep
And from barn smells you can't wash out of plowed ground
With all the rain and snow of seven years;

And I don't mean just skulls of Rogers' Rangers
On Moosilauke, but woman signs to man,
Only bewitched so I would last him longer.
Up where the trees grow short, the mosses tall,
I made him gather me wet snow berries
On slippery rocks beside a waterfall.
I made him do it for me in the dark.
And he liked everything I made him do.
I hope if he is where he sees me now
He's so far off he can't see what I've come to.
You *can* come down from everything to nothing.
All is, if I'd a-known when I was young
And full of it, that this would be the end,
It doesn't seem as if I'd had the courage
To make so free and kick up in folks' faces.
I might have, but it doesn't seem as if.

AN EMPTY THREAT

I stay;
But it isn't as if
There wasn't always Hudson's Bay
And the fur trade,
A small skiff
And a paddle blade.

I can just see my tent pegged,
And me on the floor,
Crosslegged,
And a trapper looking in at the door
With furs to sell.

His name's Joe, ·
Alias John,
And between what he doesn't know
And won't tell
About where Henry Hudson's gone,
I can't say he's much help;
But we get on.

The seal yelp
On an ice cake.
It's not men by some mistake?

No,
There's not a soul
For a wind-break
'Between me and the North Pole—

Except always John-Joe,
My French Indian Esquimaux,
And he's off setting traps,
In one himself perhaps.

Give a head shake
Over so much bay
Thrown away
In snow and mist
That doesn't exist,
I was going to say,
For God, man or beast's sake,
Yet does perhaps for all three.

Don't ask Joe
What it is to him.

It's sometimes dim
What it is to me,
Unless it be
It's the old captain's dark fate
Who failed to find or force a strait
In its two-thousand-mile coast;
And his crew left him where he failed,
And nothing came of all he sailed.

It's to say, 'You and I'
To such a ghost,
'You and I
Off here
With the dead race of the Great Auk!'
And, 'Better defeat almost,
If seen clear,
Than life's victories of doubt
That need endless talk talk
To make them out.'

FRAGMENTARY BLUE

Why make so much of fragmentary blue
In here and there a bird, or butterfly,
Or flower, or wearing-stone, or open eye,
When heaven presents in sheets the solid hue?

Since earth is earth, perhaps, not heaven (as yet)—
Though some savants make earth include the sky;
And blue so far above us comes so high,
It only gives our wish for blue a whet.

FIRE AND ICE

Some say the world will end in fire,
Some say in ice.
From what I've tasted of desire
I hold with those who favor fire.
But if it had to perish twice,
I think I know enough of hate
To say that for destruction ice
Is also great
And would suffice.

IN A DISUSED GRAVEYARD

The living come with grassy tread
To read the gravestones on the hill;
The graveyard draws the living still,
But never any more the dead.

The verses in it say and say:
'The ones who living come today
To read the stones and go away
Tomorrow dead will come to stay.'

So sure of death the marbles rhyme,
Yet can't help marking all the time
How no one dead will seem to come.
What is it men are shrinking from?

It would be easy to be clever
And tell the stones: Men hate to die
And have stopped dying now forever.
I think they would believe the lie.

DUST OF SNOW

The way a crow
Shook down on me
The dust of snow
From a hemlock tree

Has given my heart
A change of mood
And saved some part
Of a day I had rued.

NOTHING GOLD CAN STAY

Nature's first green is gold,
Her hardest hue to hold.
Her early leaf's a flower;
But only so an hour.
Then leaf subsides to leaf.
So Eden sank to grief,
So dawn goes down to day.
Nothing gold can stay.

THE RUNAWAY

Once when the snow of the year was beginning to fall,
We stopped by a mountain pasture to say, 'Whose colt?'
A little Morgan had one forefoot on the wall,
The other curled at his breast. He dipped his head
And snorted at us. And then he had to bolt.
We heard the miniature thunder where he fled,
And we saw him, or thought we saw him, dim and gray,

Like a shadow against the curtain of falling flakes.
'I think the little fellow's afraid of the snow.
He isn't winter-broken. It isn't play
With the little fellow at all. He's running away.
I doubt if even his mother could tell him, "Sakes,
It's only weather." He'd think she didn't know!
Where is his mother? He can't be out alone.'
And now he comes again with clatter of stone,
And mounts the wall again with whited eyes
And all his tail that isn't hair up straight.
He shudders his coat as if to throw off flies.
'Whoever it is that leaves him out so late,
When other creatures have gone to stall and bin,
Ought to be told to come and take him in.'

THE AIM WAS SONG

Before man came to blow it right
    The wind once blew itself untaught,
And did its loudest day and night
    In any rough place where it caught.

Man came to tell it what was wrong:
    It hadn't found the place to blow;
It blew too hard—the aim was song.
    And listen—how it ought to go!

He took a little in his mouth,
    And held it long enough for north
To be converted into south,
    And then by measure blew it forth.

By measure. It was word and note,
   The wind the wind had meant to be—
A little through the lips and throat.
   The aim was song—the wind could see.

STOPPING BY WOODS ON A
SNOWY EVENING

Whose woods these are I think I know.
His house is in the village though;
He will not see me stopping here
To watch his woods fill up with snow.

My little horse must think it queer
To stop without a farmhouse near
Between the woods and frozen lake
The darkest evening of the year.

He gives his harness bells a shake
To ask if there is some mistake.
The only other sound's the sweep
Of easy wind and downy flake.

The woods are lovely, dark and deep,
But I have promises to keep,
And miles to go before I sleep,
And miles to go before I sleep.

FOR ONCE, THEN, SOMETHING

Others taunt me with having knelt at well-curbs
Always wrong to the light, so never seeing
Deeper down in the well than where the water

Gives me back in a shining surface picture
Me myself in the summer heaven godlike
Looking out of a wreath of fern and cloud puffs.
Once, when trying with chin against a well-curb,
I discerned, as I thought, beyond the picture,
Through the picture, a something white, uncertain,
Something more of the depths—and then I lost it.
Water came to rebuke the too clear water.
One drop fell from a fern, and lo, a ripple
Shook whatever it was lay there at bottom,
Blurred it, blotted it out. What was that whiteness?
Truth? A pebble of quartz? For once, then, something.

BLUE-BUTTERFLY DAY

It is blue-butterfly day here in spring,
And with these sky-flakes down in flurry on flurry
There is more unmixed color on the wing
Than flowers will show for days unless they hurry.

But these are flowers that fly and all but sing:
And now from having ridden out desire
They lie closed over in the wind and cling
Where wheels have freshly sliced the April mire.

THE ONSET

Always the same, when on a fated night
At last the gathered snow lets down as white
As may be in dark woods, and with a song
It shall not make again all winter long
Of hissing on the yet uncovered ground,
I almost stumble looking up and round,

As one who overtaken by the end
Gives up his errand, and lets death descend
Upon him where he is, with nothing done
To evil, no important triumph won,
More than if life had never been begun.

Yet all the precedent is on my side:
I know that winter death has never tried
The earth but it has failed: the snow may heap
In long storms an undrifted four feet deep
As measured against maple, birch, and oak,
It cannot check the peeper's silver croak;
And I shall see the snow all go down hill
In water of a slender April rill
That flashes tail through last year's withered brake
And dead weeds, like a disappearing snake.
Nothing will be left white but here a birch,
And there a clump of houses with a church.

TO EARTHWARD

Love at the lips was touch
As sweet as I could bear;
And once that seemed too much;
I lived on air

That crossed me from sweet things
The flow of—was it musk
From hidden grapevine springs
Down hill at dusk?

I had the swirl and ache
From sprays of honeysuckle
That when they're gathered shake
Dew on the knuckle.

I craved strong sweets, but those
Seemed strong when I was young;
The petal of the rose
It was that stung.

Now no joy but lacks salt
That is not dashed with pain
And weariness and fault;
I crave the stain

Of tears, the aftermark
Of almost too much love,
The sweet of bitter bark
And burning clove.

When stiff and sore and scarred
I take away my hand
From leaning on it hard
In grass and sand,

The hurt is not enough:
I long for weight and strength
To feel the earth as rough
To all my length.

GOOD-BY AND KEEP COLD

This saying good-by on the edge of the dark
And the cold to an orchard so young in the bark
Reminds me of all that can happen to harm
An orchard away at the end of the farm
All winter, cut off by a hill from the house.
I don't want it girdled by rabbit and mouse,

I don't want it dreamily nibbled for browse
By deer, and I don't want it budded by grouse.
(If certain it wouldn't be idle to call
I'd summon grouse, rabbit, and deer to the wall
And warn them away with a stick for a gun.)
I don't want it stirred by the heat of the sun.
(We made it secure against being, I hope,
By setting it out on a northerly slope.)
No orchard's the worse for the wintriest storm;
But one thing about it, it mustn't get warm.
'How often already you've had to be told,
Keep cold, young orchard. Good-by and keep cold.
Dread fifty above more than fifty below.'
I have to be gone for a season or so.
My business awhile is with different trees,
Less carefully nurtured, less fruitful than these,
And such as is done to their wood with an ax—
Maples and birches and tamaracks.
I wish I could promise to lie in the night
And think of an orchard's arboreal plight
When slowly (and nobody comes with a light)
Its heart sinks lower under the sod.
But something has to be left to God.

LOOKING FOR A SUNSET BIRD
IN WINTER

The west was getting out of gold,
The breath of air had died of cold,
When shoeing home across the white,
I thought I saw a bird alight.

In summer when I passed the place
I had to stop and lift my face;
A bird with an angelic gift
Was singing in it sweet and swift.

No bird was singing in it now.
A single leaf was on a bough,
And that was all there was to see
In going twice around the tree.

From my advantage on a hill
I judged that such a crystal chill
Was only adding frost to snow
As gilt to gold that wouldn't show.

A brush had left a crooked stroke
Of what was either cloud or smoke
From north to south across the blue;
A piercing little star was through.

THE KITCHEN CHIMNEY

Builder, in building the little house,
In every way you may please yourself;
But please please me in the kitchen chimney:
Don't build me a chimney upon a shelf.

However far you must go for bricks,
Whatever they cost a-piece or a pound,
Buy me enough for a full-length chimney,
And build the chimney clear from the ground.

It's not that I'm greatly afraid of fire,
But I never heard of a house that throve
(And I know of one that didn't thrive)
Where the chimney started above the stove.

And I dread the omnious stain of tar
That there always is on the papered walls,
And the smell of fire drowned in rain
That there always is when the chimney's false.

A shelf's for a clock or vase or picture,
But I don't see why it should have to bear
A chimney that only would serve to remind me
Of castles I used to build in air.

GATHERING LEAVES

Spades take up leaves
No better than spoons,
And bags full of leaves
Are light as balloons.

I make a great noise
Of rustling all day
Like rabbit and deer
Running away.

But the mountains I raise
Elude my embrace,
Flowing over my arms
And into my face.

I may load and unload
Again and again
Till I fill the whole shed,
And what have I then?

Next to nothing for weight,
And since they grew duller
From contact with earth,
Next to nothing for color.

Next to nothing for use.
But a crop is a crop,
And who's to say where
The harvest shall stop?

MISGIVING

All crying, 'We will go with you, O Wind!'
The foliage follow him, leaf and stem;
But a sleep oppresses them as they go,
And they end by bidding him stay with them.

Since ever they flung abroad in spring
The leaves had promised themselves this flight,
Who now would fain seek sheltering wall,
Or thicket, or hollow place for the night.

And now they answer his summoning blast
With an ever vaguer and vaguer stir,
Or at utmost a little reluctant whirl
That drops them no further than where they were.

I only hope that when I am free
As they are free to go in quest
Of the knowledge beyond the bounds of life
It may not seem better to me to rest.

ON A TREE FALLEN ACROSS THE ROAD

(To hear us talk)

The tree the tempest with a crash of wood
Throws down in front of us is not to bar
Our passage to our journey's end for good,
But just to ask us who we think we are

Insisting always on our own way so.
She likes to halt us in our runner tracks,
And make us get down in a foot of snow
Debating what to do without an ax.

And yet she knows obstruction is in vain:
We will not be put off the final goal
We have it hidden in us to attain,
Not though we have to seize earth by the pole

And, tired of aimless circling in one place,
Steer straight off after something into space.

OUR SINGING STRENGTH

It snowed in spring on earth so dry and warm
The flakes could find no landing place to form.
Hordes spent themselves to make it wet and cold,
And still they failed of any lasting hold.
They made no white impression on the black.
They disappeared as if earth sent them back.
Not till from separate flakes they changed at night
To almost strips and tapes of ragged white
Did grass and garden ground confess it snowed,

And all go back to winter but the road.
Next day the scene was piled and puffed and dead.
The grass lay flattened under one great tread.
Borne down until the end almost took root,
The rangey bough anticipated fruit
With snowballs cupped in every opening bud.
The road alone maintained itself in mud,
Whatever its secret was of greater heat
From inward fires or brush of passing feet.

In spring more mortal singers than belong
To any one place cover us with song.
Thrush, bluebird, blackbird, sparrow, and robin throng;
Some to go further north to Hudson's Bay,
Some that have come too far north back away,
Really a very few to build and stay.
Now was seen how these liked belated snow.
The fields had nowhere left for them to go;
They'd soon exhausted all there was in flying;
The trees they'd had enough of with once trying
And setting off their heavy powder load.
They could find nothing open but the road.
So there they let their lives be narrowed in
By thousands the bad weather made akin.
The road became a channel running flocks
Of glossy birds like ripples over rocks.
I drove them under foot in bits of flight
That kept the ground, almost disputing right
Of way with me from apathy of wing,
A talking twitter all they had to sing.
A few I must have driven to despair
Made quick asides, but having done in air
A whir among white branches great and small
As in some too much carven marble hall

Where one false wing beat would have brought down all,
Came tamely back in front of me, the Drover,
To suffer the same driven nightmare over.
One such storm in a lifetime couldn't teach them
That back behind pursuit it couldn't reach them;
None flew behind me to be left alone.

Well, something for a snowstorm to have shown
The country's singing strength thus brought together,
That though repressed and moody with the weather
Was none the less there ready to be freed
And sing the wildflowers up from root and seed.

THE LOCKLESS DOOR

It went many years,
But at last came a knock,
And I thought of the door
With no lock to lock.

I blew out the light,
I tip-toed the floor,
And raised both hands
In prayer to the door.

But the knock came again
My window was wide;
I climbed on the sill
And descended outside.

Back over the sill
I bade a 'Come in'
To whatever the knock
At the door may have been.

So at a knock
I emptied my cage
To hide in the world
And alter with age.

THE NEED OF BEING VERSED IN
COUNTRY THINGS

The house had gone to bring again
To the midnight sky a sunset glow.
Now the chimney was all of the house that stood,
Like a pistil after the petals go.

The barn opposed across the way,
That would have joined the house in flame
Had it been the will of the wind, was left
To bear forsaken the place's name.

No more it opened with all one end
For teams that came by the stony road
To drum on the floor with scurrying hoofs
And brush the mow with the summer load.

The birds that came to it through the air
At broken windows flew out and in,
Their murmur more like the sigh we sigh
From too much dwelling on what has been.

Yet for them the lilac renewed its leaf,
And the aged elm, though touched with fire;
And the dry pump flung up an awkward arm;
And the fence post carried a strand of wire.

New Hampshire

For them there was really nothing sad.
But though they rejoiced in the nest they kept,
One had to be versed in country things
Not to believe the phoebes wept.

West-running Brook

SPRING POOLS

These pools that, though in forests, still reflect
The total sky almost without defect,
And like the flowers beside them, chill and shiver,
Will like the flowers beside them soon be gone,
And yet not out by any brook or river,
But up by roots to bring dark foliage on.

The trees that have it in their pent-up buds
To darken nature and be summer woods—
Let them think twice before they use their powers
To blot out and drink up and sweep away
These flowery waters and these watery flowers
From snow that melted only yesterday.

FIREFLIES IN THE GARDEN

Here come real stars to fill the upper skies,
And here on earth come emulating flies,
That though they never equal stars in size,

(And they were never really stars at heart)
Achieve at times a very star-like start.
Only, of course, they can't sustain the part.

DEVOTION

The heart can think of no devotion
Greater than being shore to the ocean—
Holding the curve of one position,
Counting an endless repetition.

ON GOING UNNOTICED

As vain to raise a voice as a sigh
In the tumult of free leaves on high.
What are you in the shadow of trees
Engaged up there with the light and breeze?

Less than the coral-root you know
That is content with the daylight low,
And has no leaves at all of its own;
Whose spotted flowers hang meanly down.

You grasp the bark by a rugged pleat,
And look up small from the forest's feet.
The only leaf it drops goes wide,
Your name not written on either side.

You linger your little hour and are gone,
And still the woods sweep leafily on,
Not even missing the coral-root flower
You took as a trophy of the hour.

A PASSING GLIMPSE

To Ridgely Torrence
On Last Looking into His 'Hesperides'

I often see flowers from a passing car
That are gone before I can tell what they are.

I want to get out of the train and go back
To see what they were beside the track.

I name all the flowers I am sure they weren't:
Not fireweed loving where woods have burnt—

Not bluebells gracing a tunnel mouth—
Not lupine living on sand and drouth.

Was something brushed across my mind
That no one on earth will ever find?

Heaven gives its glimpses only to those
Not in position to look too close.

A PECK OF GOLD

Dust always blowing about the town,
Except when sea-fog laid it down,
And I was one of the children told
Some of the blowing dust was gold.

All the dust the wind blew high
Appeared like gold in the sunset sky,
But I was one of the children told
Some of the dust was really gold.

Such was life in the Golden Gate:
Gold dusted all we drank and ate,
And I was one of the children told,
'We all must eat our peck of gold.'

ACCEPTANCE

When the spent sun throws up its rays on cloud
And goes down burning into the gulf below,
No voice in nature is heard to cry aloud
At what has happened. Birds, at least, must know
It is the change to darkness in the sky.
Murmuring something quiet in her breast,
One bird begins to close a faded eye;
Or overtaken too far from his nest,
Hurrying low above the grove, some waif
Swoops just in time to his remembered tree.
At most he thinks or twitters softly, 'Safe!
Now let the night be dark for all of me.
Let the night be too dark for me to see
Into the future. Let what will be, be.'

ONCE BY THE PACIFIC

The shattered water made a misty din.
Great waves looked over others coming in,
And thought of doing something to the shore
That water never did to land before.
The clouds were low and hairy in the skies,
Like locks blown forward in the gleam of eyes.
You could not tell, and yet it looked as if

The shore was lucky in being backed by cliff,
The cliff in being backed by continent;
It looked as if a night of dark intent
Was coming, and not only a night, an age.
Someone had better be prepared for rage.
There would be more than ocean-water broken
Before God's last *Put out the Light* was spoken.

LODGED

The rain to the wind said,
'You push and I'll pelt.'
They so smote the garden bed
That the flowers actually knelt,
And lay lodged—though not dead.
I know how the flowers felt.

A MINOR BIRD

I have wished a bird would fly away,
And not sing by my house all day;

Have clapped my hands at him from the door
When it seemed as if I could bear no more.

The fault must partly have been in me.
The bird was not to blame for his key.

And of course there must be something wrong
In wanting to silence any song.

BEREFT

Where had I heard this wind before
Change like this to a deeper roar?
What would it take my standing there for,
Holding open a restive door,
Looking down hill to a frothy shore?
Summer was past and day was past.
Somber clouds in the west were massed.
Out in the porch's sagging floor,
Leaves got up in a coil and hissed,
Blindly struck at my knee and missed.
Something sinister in the tone
Told me my secret must be known:
Word I was in the house alone
Somehow must have gotten abroad,
Word I was in my life alone,
Word I had no one left but God.

TREE AT MY WINDOW

Tree at my window, window tree,
My sash is lowered when night comes on;
But let there never be curtain drawn
Between you and me.

Vague dream-head lifted out of the ground,
And thing next most diffuse to cloud,
Not all your light tongues talking aloud
Could be profound.

But, tree, I have seen you taken and tossed,
And if you have seen me when I slept,
You have seen me when I was taken and swept
And all but lost.

That day she put our heads together,
Fate had her imagination about her,
Your head so much concerned with outer,
Mine with inner, weather.

THE PEACEFUL SHEPHERD

If heaven were to do again,
And on the pasture bars,
I leaned to line the figures in
Between the dotted stars,

I should be tempted to forget,
I fear, the Crown of Rule,
The Scales of Trade, the Cross of Faith,
As hardly worth renewal.

For these have governed in our lives,
And see how men have warred.
The Cross, the Crown, the Scales may all
As well have been the Sword.

A WINTER EDEN

A winter garden in an alder swamp,
Where conies now come out to sun and romp,
As near a paradise as it can be
And not melt snow or start a dormant tree.

It lifts existence on a plane of snow
One level higher than the earth below,
One level nearer heaven overhead,
And last year's berries shining scarlet red.

It lifts a gaunt luxuriating beast
Where he can stretch and hold his highest feast
On some wild apple tree's young tender bark,
What well may prove the year's high girdle mark.

So near to paradise all pairing ends:
Here loveless birds now flock as winter friends,
Content with bud-inspecting. They presume
To say which buds are leaf and which are bloom.

A feather-hammer gives a double knock.
This Eden day is done at two o'clock.
An hour of winter day might seem too short
To make it worth life's while to wake and sport.

THE FLOOD

Blood has been harder to dam back than water.
Just when we think we have it impounded safe
Behind new barrier walls (and let it chafe!),
It breaks away in some new kind of slaughter.
We choose to say it is let loose by the devil;
But power of blood itself releases blood.
It goes by might of being such a flood
Held high at so unnatural a level.
It will have outlet, brave and not so brave.
Weapons of war and implements of peace
Are but the points at which it finds release.
And now it is once more the tidal wave
That when it has swept by leaves summits stained.
Oh, blood will out. It cannot be contained.

ACQUAINTED WITH THE NIGHT

I have been one acquainted with the night.
I have walked out in rain—and back in rain.
I have outwalked the furthest city light.

I have looked down the saddest city lane.
I have passed by the watchman on his beat
And dropped my eyes, unwilling to explain.

I have stood still and stopped the sound of feet
When far away an interrupted cry
Came over houses from another street,

But not to call me back or say good-by;
And further still at an unearthly height,
One luminary clock against the sky

Proclaimed the time was neither wrong nor right.
I have been one acquainted with the night.

THE LOVELY SHALL BE CHOOSERS

The Voice said, 'Hurl her down!'

The Voices, 'How far down?'

'Seven levels of the world.'

'How much time have we?'

'Take twenty years.
She *would* refuse love safe with wealth and honor!
The lovely shall be choosers, shall they?
Then let them choose!'

'Then we shall let her choose?'

'Yes, let her choose.
Take up the task beyond her choosing.'

Invisible hands crowded on her shoulder
In readiness to weigh upon her.
But she stood straight still,
In broad round ear-rings, gold and jet with pearls
And broad round suchlike brooch,
Her cheeks high colored,
Proud and the pride of friends.

The Voice asked, 'You can let her choose?'

'Yes, we can let her and still triumph.'

'Do it by joys, and leave her always blameless.
Be her first joy her wedding,
That though a wedding,
Is yet—well something they know, he and she.
And after that her next joy
That though she grieves, her grief is secret:
Those friends know nothing of her grief to make it shameful.
Her third joy that though now they cannot help but know,
They move in pleasure too far off
To think much or much care.
Give her a child at either knee for fourth joy
To tell once and once only, for them never to forget,
How once she walked in brightness,
And make them see it in the winter firelight.
But give her friends for then she dare not tell
For their foregone incredulousness.
And be her next joy this:
Her never having deigned to tell them.
Make her among the humblest even

Seem to them less than they are.
Hopeless of being known for what she has been,
Failing of being loved for what she is,
Give her the comfort for her sixth of knowing
She fails from strangeness to a way of life
She came to from too high too late to learn.
Then send some *one* with eyes to see
And wonder at her where she is,
And words to wonder in her hearing how she came there,
But without time to linger for her story.
Be her last joy her heart's going out to this one
So that she almost speaks.
You know them—seven in all.'

'Trust us,' the Voices said.

WEST-RUNNING BROOK

'Fred, where is north?'

                        'North? North is there, my love.
The brook runs west.'

                        'West-running Brook then call it.'
(West-running Brook men call it to this day.)
'What does it think it's doing running west
When all the other country brooks flow east
To reach the ocean? It must be the brook
Can trust itself to go by contraries
The way I can with you—and you with me—
Because we're—we're—I don't know what we are.
What are we?'

                'Young or new?'

                         'We must be something.
We've said we two. Let's change that to we three.
As you and I are married to each other,
We'll both be married to the brook. We'll build
Our bridge across it, and the bridge shall be
Our arm thrown over it asleep beside it.
Look, look, it's waving to us with a wave
To let us know it hears me.'

                    'Why, my dear,
That wave's been standing off this jut of shore—'
(The black stream, catching on a sunken rock,
Flung backward on itself in one white wave,
And the white water rode the black forever,
Not gaining but not losing, like a bird
White feathers from the struggle of whose breast
Flecked the dark stream and flecked the darker pool
Below the point, and were at last driven wrinkled
In a white scarf against the far shore alders.)
'That wave's been standing off this jut of shore
Ever since rivers, I was going to say,
Were made in heaven. It wasn't waved to us.'

'It wasn't, yet it was. If not to you
It was to me—in an annunciation.'

'Oh, if you take it off to lady-land,
As't were the country of the Amazons
We men must see you to the confines of
And leave you there, ourselves forbid to enter,—
It is your brook! I have no more to say.'

'Yes, you have, too. Go on. You thought of something.'

'Speaking of contraries, see how the brook

In that white wave runs counter to itself.
It is from that in water we were from
Long, long before we were from any creature.
Here we, in our impatience of the steps,
Get back to the beginning of beginnings,
The stream of everything that runs away.
Some say existence like a Pirouot
And Pirouette, forever in one place,
Stands still and dances, but it runs away,
It seriously, sadly, runs away
To fill the abyss' void with emptiness.
It flows beside us in this water brook,
But it flows over us. It flows between us
To separate us for a panic moment.
It flows between us, over us, and *with* us.
And it is time, strength, tone, light, life, and love—
And even substance lapsing unsubstantial;
The universal cataract of death
That spends to nothingness—and unresisted,
Save by some strange resistance in itself,
Not just a swerving, but a throwing back,
As if regret were in it and were sacred.
It has this throwing backward on itself
So that the fall of most of it is always
Raising a little, sending up a little.
Our life runs down in sending up the clock.
The brook runs down in sending up our life.
The sun runs down in sending up the brook.
And there is something sending up the sun.
It is this backward motion toward the source,
Against the stream, that most we see ourselves in,
The tribute of the current to the source.
It is from this in nature we are from.
It is most us.'

'Today will be the day
You said so.'

'No, today will be the day
You said the brook was called West-running Brook.'

'Today will be the day of what we both said.'

SAND DUNES

Sea waves are green and wet,
But up from where they die,
Rise others vaster yet,
And those are brown and dry.

They are the sea made land
To come at the fisher town,
And bury in solid sand
The men she could not drown.

She may know cove and cape,
But she does not know mankind
If by any change of shape,
She hopes to cut off mind.

Men left her a ship to sink:
They can leave her a hut as well;
And be but more free to think
For the one more cast-off shell.

CANIS MAJOR

The great Overdog.
That heavenly beast
With a star in one eye,
Gives a leap in the east.

He dances upright
All the way to the west
And never once drops
On his forefeet to rest.

I'm a poor underdog,
But tonight I will bark
With the great Overdog
That romps through the dark.

A SOLDIER

He is that fallen lance that lies as hurled,
That lies unlifted now, come dew, come rust,
But still lies pointed as it plowed the dust.
If we who sight along it round the world,
See nothing worthy to have been its mark,
It is because like men we look too near,
Forgetting that as fitted to the sphere,
Our missiles always make too short an arc.
They fall, they rip the grass, they intersect
The curve of earth, and striking, break their own;
They make us cringe for metal-point on stone.
But this we know, the obstacle that checked
And tripped the body, shot the spirit on
Further than target ever showed or shone.

IMMIGRANTS

No ship of all that under sail or steam
Have gathered people to us more and more
But Pilgrim-manned the *Mayflower* in a dream
Has been her anxious convoy in to shore.

HANNIBAL

Was there ever a cause too lost,
Ever a cause that was lost too long,
Or that showed with the lapse of time too vain
For the generous tears of youth and song?

THE TIMES TABLE

More than halfway up the pass
Was a spring with a broken drinking glass,
And whether the farmer drank or not
His mare was sure to observe the spot
By cramping the wheel on a water-bar,
Turning her forehead with a star,
And straining her ribs for a monster sigh;
To which the farmer would make reply,
'A sigh for every so many breath,
And for every so many sigh a death.
That's what I always tell my wife
Is the multiplication table of life.'
The saying may be ever so true;
But it's just the kind of a thing that you
Nor I, nor nobody else may say,
Unless our purpose is doing harm,

And then I know of no better way
To close a road, abandon a farm,
Reduce the births of the human race,
And bring back nature in people's place.

THE INVESTMENT

Over back where they speak of life as staying
('You couldn't call it living, for it ain't'),
There was an old, old house renewed with paint,
And in it a piano loudly playing.

Out in the plowed ground in the cold a digger,
Among unearthed potatoes standing still,
Was counting winter dinners, one a hill,
With half an ear to the piano's vigor.

All that piano and new paint back there,
Was it some money suddenly come into?
Or some extravagance young love had been to?
Or old love on an impulse not to care—

Not to sink under being man and wife,
But get some color and music out of life?

THE LAST MOWING

There's a place called Far-away Meadow
We never shall mow in again,
Or such is the talk at the farmhouse:

The meadow is finished with men.
Then now is the chance for the flowers
That can't stand mowers and plowers.
It must be now, though, in season
Before the not mowing brings trees on,
Before trees, seeing the opening,
March into a shadowy claim.
The trees are all I'm afraid of,
That flowers can't bloom in the shade of;
It's no more men I'm afraid of;
The meadow is done with the tame.
The place for the moment is ours
For you, oh tumultuous flowers,
To go to waste and go wild in,
All shapes and colors of flowers,
I needn't call you by name.

THE BIRTHPLACE

Here further up the mountain slope
Than there was ever any hope,
My father built, enclosed a spring,
Strung chains of wall round everything,
Subdued the growth of earth to grass,
And brought our various lives to pass.
A dozen girls and boys we were.
The mountain seemed to like the stir,
And made of us a little while—
With always something in her smile.
Today she wouldn't know our name.
(No girl's, of course, has stayed the same.)
The mountain pushed us off her knees.
And now her lap is full of trees.

DUST IN THE EYES

If, as they say, some dust thrown in my eyes
Will keep my talk from getting overwise,
I'm not the one for putting off the proof.
Let it be overwhelming, off a roof
And round a corner, blizzard snow for dust,
And blind me to a standstill if it must.

SITTING BY A BUSH
IN BROAD SUNLIGHT

When I spread out my hand here today,
I catch no more than a ray
To feel of between thumb and fingers;
No lasting effect of it lingers.

There was one time and only the one
When dust really took in the sun;
And from that one intake of fire
All creatures still warmly suspire.

And if men have watched a long time
And never seen sun-smitten slime
Again come to life and crawl off,
We must not be too ready to scoff.

God once declared he was true
And then took the veil and withdrew,
And remember how final a hush
Then descended of old on the bush.

God once spoke to people by name.
The sun once imparted its flame.
One impulse persists as our breath;
The other persists as our faith.

THE ARMFUL

For every parcel I stoop down to seize,
I lose some other off my arms and knees,
And the whole pile is slipping, bottles, buns,
Extremes too hard to comprehend at once,
Yet nothing I should care to leave behind.
With all I have to hold with, hand and mind
And heart, if need be, I will do my best
To keep their building balanced at my breast.
I crouch down to prevent them as they fall;
Then sit down in the middle of them all.
I had to drop the armful in the road
And try to stack them in a better load.

WHAT FIFTY SAID

When I was young my teachers were the old.
I gave up fire for form till I was cold.
I suffered like a metal being cast.
I went to school to age to learn the past.

Now I am old my teachers are the young.
What can't be molded must be cracked and sprung.
I strain at lessons fit to start a suture.
I go to school to youth to learn the future.

RIDERS

The surest thing there is is we are riders,
And though none too successful at it, guiders,
Through everything presented, land and tide
And now the very air, of what we ride.

What is this talked-of mystery of birth
But being mounted bareback on the earth?
We can just see the infant up astride,
His small fist buried in the bushy hide.

There is our wildest mount—a headless horse.
But though it runs unbridled off its course,
And all our blandishments would seem defied,
We have ideas yet that we haven't tried.

ON LOOKING UP BY CHANCE AT THE CONSTELLATIONS

You'll wait a long, long time for anything much
To happen in heaven beyond the floats of cloud
And the Northern Lights that run like tingling nerves.
The sun and moon get crossed, but they never touch,
Nor strike out fire from each other, nor crash out loud.
The planets seem to interfere in their curves,
But nothing ever happens, no harm is done.
We may as well go patiently on with our life,
And look elsewhere than to stars and moon and sun
For the shocks and changes we need to keep us sane.
It is true the longest drouth will end in rain,
The longest peace in China will end in strife.

Still it wouldn't reward the watcher to stay awake
In hopes of seeing the calm of heaven break
On his particular time and personal sight.
That calm seems certainly safe to last tonight.

THE BEAR

The bear puts both arms around the tree above her
And draws it down as if it were a lover
And its choke cherries lips to kiss good-by,
Then lets it snap back upright in the sky.
Her next step rocks a boulder on the wall
(She's making her cross-country in the fall).
Her great weight creaks the barbed-wire in its staples
As she flings over and off down through the maples,
Leaving on one wire tooth a lock of hair.
Such is the uncaged progress of the bear.
The world has room to make a bear feel free;
The universe seems cramped to you and me.
Man acts more like the poor bear in a cage
That all day fights a nervous inward rage,
His mood rejecting all his mind suggests.
He paces back and forth and never rests
The toe-nail click and shuffle of his feet,
The telescope at one end of his beat,
And at the other end the microscope,
Two instruments of nearly equal hope,
And in conjunction giving quite a spread.
Or if he rests from scientific tread,
'Tis only to sit back and sway his head
Through ninety odd degrees of arc, it seems,
Between two metaphysical extremes.
He sits back on his fundamental butt

The Bear

With lifted snout and eyes (if any) shut,
(He almost looks religious but he's not),
And back and forth he sways from cheek to cheek,
At one extreme agreeing with one Greek,
At the other agreeing with another Greek
Which may be thought, but only so to speak.
A baggy figure, equally pathetic
When sedentary and when peripatetic.

A Further Range

TAKEN DOUBLY

A LONE STRIKER

The swinging mill bell changed its rate
To tolling like the count of fate,
And though at that the tardy ran,
One failed to make the closing gate.
There was a law of God or man
That on the one who came too late
The gate for half an hour be locked,
His time be lost, his pittance docked.
He stood rebuked and unemployed.
The straining mill began to shake.
The mill, though many, many eyed,
Had eyes inscrutably opaque;
So that he couldn't look inside
To see if some forlorn machine
Was standing idle for his sake.
(He couldn't hope its heart would break.)

And yet he thought he saw the scene:
The air was full of dust of wool.
A thousand yarns were under pull,
But pull so slow, with such a twist,
All day from spool to lesser spool,
It seldom overtaxed their strength;
They safely grew in slender length.
And if one broke by any chance,
The spinner saw it at a glance.
The spinner still was there to spin.

That's where the human still came in.
Her deft hand showed with finger rings
Among the harp-like spread of strings.
She caught the pieces end to end
And, with a touch that never missed,
Not so much tied as made them blend.
Man's ingenuity was good.
He saw it plainly where he stood,
Yet found it easy to resist.

He knew another place, a wood,
And in it, tall as trees, were cliffs;
And if he stood on one of these,
'Twould be among the tops of trees,
Their upper branches round him wreathing,
Their breathing mingled with his breathing.
If—if he stood! Enough of ifs!
He knew a path that wanted walking;
He knew a spring that wanted drinking;
A thought that wanted further thinking;
A love that wanted re-renewing.
Nor was this just a way of talking

To save him the expense of doing.
With him it boded action, deed.

The factory was very fine;
He wished it all the modern speed.
Yet, after all, 'twas not divine,
That is to say, 'twas not a church.
He never would assume that he'd
Be any institution's need.
But he said then and still would say
If there should ever come a day
When industry seemed like to die
Because he left it in the lurch,
Or even merely seemed to pine
For want of his approval, why,
Come get him—they knew where to search.

TWO TRAMPS IN MUD TIME

Out of the mud two strangers came
And caught me splitting wood in the yard.
And one of them put me off my aim
By hailing cheerily 'Hit them hard!'
I knew pretty well why he dropped behind
And let the other go on a way.
I knew pretty well what he had in mind:
He wanted to take my job for pay.

Good blocks of oak it was I split,
As large around as the chopping block;
And every piece I squarely hit
Fell splinterless as a cloven rock.
The blows that a life of self-control

Two Tramps in Mud Time

Spares to strike for the common good
That day, giving a loose to my soul,
I spent on the unimportant wood.

The sun was warm but the wind was chill.
You know how it is with an April day
When the sun is out and the wind is still,
You're one month on in the middle of May.
But if you so much as dare to speak,
A cloud comes over the sunlit arch,
A wind comes off a frozen peak,
And you're two months back in the middle of March.

A bluebird comes tenderly up to alight
And turns to the wind to unruffle a plume
His song so pitched as not to excite
A single flower as yet to bloom.

It is snowing a flake: and he half knew
Winter was only playing possum.
Except in color he isn't blue,
But he wouldn't advise a thing to blossom.

The water for which we may have to look
In summertime with a witching-wand,
In every wheelrut's now a brook,
In every print of a hoof a pond.
Be glad of water, but don't forget
The lurking frost in the earth beneath
That will steal forth after the sun is set
And show on the water its crystal teeth.

The time when most I loved my task
These two must make me love it more
By coming with what they came to ask.

You'd think I never had felt before
The weight of an ax-head poised aloft,
The grip on earth of outspread feet.
The life of muscles rocking soft
And smooth and moist in vernal heat.

Out of the woods two hulking tramps
(From sleeping God knows where last night,
But not long since in the lumber camps).
They thought all chopping was theirs of right.
Men of the woods and lumberjacks,
They judged me by their appropriate tool.
Except as a fellow handled an ax,
They had no way of knowing a fool.

Nothing on either side was said.
They knew they had but to stay their stay
And all their logic would fill my head:
As that I had no right to play
With what was another man's work for gain.
My right might be love but theirs was need.
And where the two exist in twain
Theirs was the better right—agreed.

But yield who will to their separation,
My object in living is to unite
My avocation and my vocation
As my two eyes make one in sight.
Only where love and need are one,
And the work is play for mortal stakes,
Is the deed ever really done
For Heaven and the future's sakes.

THE WHITE-TAILED HORNET

The white-tailed hornet lives in a balloon
That floats against the ceiling of the woodshed.
The exit he comes out at like a bullet
Is like the pupil of a pointed gun.
And having power to change his aim in flight,
He comes out more unerring than a bullet.
Verse could be written on the certainty
With which he penetrates my best defense
Of whirling hands and arms about the head
To stab me in the sneeze-nerve of a nostril.
Such is the instinct of it I allow.
Yet how about the insect certainty
That in the neighborhood of home and children
Is such an execrable judge of motives
As not to recognize in me the exception
I like to think I am in everything—
One who would never hang above a bookcase
His Japanese crepe-paper globe for trophy?
He stung me first and stung me afterward.
He rolled me off the field head over heels,
And would not listen to my explanations.

That's when I went as visitor to his house.
As visitor at my house he is better.
Hawking for flies about the kitchen door,
In at one door perhaps and out another,
Trust him then not to put you in the wrong.
He won't misunderstand your freest movements.
Let him light on your skin unless you mind
So many prickly grappling feet at once.
He's after the domesticated fly
To feed his thumping grubs as big as he is.

Here he is at his best, but even here—
I watched him where he swooped, he pounced, he struck;
But what he found he had was just a nailhead.
He struck a second time. Another nailhead.
'Those are just nailheads. Those are fastened down.'
Then disconcerted and not unannoyed,
He stooped and struck a little huckleberry
The way a player curls around a football.
'Wrong shape, wrong color, and wrong scent,' I said.
The huckleberry rolled him on his head.
At last it was a fly. He shot and missed;
And the fly circled round him in derision.
But for the fly he might have made me think
He had been at his poetry, comparing
Nailhead with fly and fly with huckleberry:
How like a fly, how very like a fly.
But the real fly he missed would never do;
The missed fly made me dangerously skeptic.

Won't this whole instinct matter bear revision?
Won't almost any theory bear revision?
To err is human, not to, animal.
Or so we pay the compliment to instinct,
Only too liberal of our compliment
That really takes away instead of gives.
Our worship, humor, conscientiousness
Went long since to the dogs under the table.
And served us right for having instituted
Downward comparisons. As long on earth
As our comparisons were stoutly upward
With gods and angels, we were men at least,
But little lower than the gods and angels.
But once comparisons were yielded downward,
Once we began to see our images

Reflected in the mud and even dust,
'Twas disillusion upon disillusion.
We were lost piecemeal to the animals,
Like people thrown out to delay the wolves.
Nothing but fallibility was left us,
And this day's work made even that seem doubtful.

A BLUE RIBBON AT AMESBURY

Such a fine pullet ought to go
All coiffured to a winter show,
And be exhibited, and win.
The answer is this one has been—

And come with all her honors home.
Her golden leg, her coral comb,
Her fluff of plumage, white as chalk,
Her style, were all the fancy's talk.

It seems as if you must have heard.
She scored an almost perfect bird.
In her we make ourselves acquainted
With one a Sewell might have painted

Here common with the flock again,
At home in her abiding pen,
She lingers feeding at the trough,
The last to let night drive her off.

The one who gave her ankle-band,
Her keeper, empty pail in hand,
He lingers too, averse to slight
His chores for all the wintry night.

He leans against the dusty wall,
Immured almost beyond recall,
A depth past many swinging doors
And many litter-muffled floors.

He meditates the breeder's art.
He has a half a mind to start,
With her for Mother Eve, a race
That shall all living things displace.

'Tis ritual with her to lay
The full six days, then rest a day;
At which rate barring broodiness
She well may score an egg-success.

The gatherer can always tell
Her well-turned egg's brown sturdy shell,
As safe a vehicle of seed
As is vouchsafed to feathered breed.

No human specter at the feast
Can scant or hurry her the least.
She takes her time to take her fill.
She whets a sleepy sated bill.

She gropes across the pen alone
To peck herself a precious stone.
She waters at the patent fount.
And so to roost, the last to mount.

The roost is her extent of flight.
Yet once she rises to the height,
She shoulders with a wing so strong
She makes the whole flock move along.

The night is setting in to blow.
It scours the windowpane with snow,
But barely gets from them or her
For comment a complacent chirr.

The lowly pen is yet a hold
Against the dark and wind and cold
To give a prospect to a plan
And warrant prudence in a man.

A DRUMLIN WOODCHUCK

One thing has a shelving bank,
Another a rotting plank,
To give it cozier skies
And make up for its lack of size.

My own strategic retreat
Is where two rocks almost meet,
And still more secure and snug,
A two-door burrow I dug.

With those in mind at my back
I can sit forth exposed to attack
As one who shrewdly pretends
That he and the world are friends.

All we who prefer to live
Have a little whistle we give,
And flash, at the least alarm
We dive down under the farm.

We allow some time for guile
And don't come out for a while
Either to eat or drink.
We take occasion to think.

And if after the hunt goes past
And the double-barreled blast
(Like war and pestilence
And the loss of common sense),

If I can with confidence say
That still for another day,
Or even another year,
I will be there for you, my dear,

It will be because, though small
As measured against the All,
I have been so instinctively thorough
About my crevice and burrow.

IN TIME OF CLOUDBURST

Let the downpour roil and toil!
The worst it can do to me
Is carry some garden soil
A little nearer the sea.

Tis the world-old way of the rain
When it comes to a mountain farm
To exact for a present gain
A little of future harm.

And the harm is none too sure,
For when all that was rotted rich
Shall be in the end scoured poor,
When my garden has gone down ditch,

Some force has but to apply,
And summits shall be immersed,
The bottom of seas raised dry—
The slope of the earth reversed.

Then all I need do is run
To the other end of the slope,
And on tracts laid new to the sun,
Begin all over to hope.

Some worn old tool of my own
Will be turned up by the plow,
The wood of it changed to stone,
But as ready to wield as now.

May my application so close
To so endless a repetition
Not make me tired and morose
And resentful of man's condition.

DEPARTMENTAL

An ant on the tablecloth
Ran into a dormant moth
Of many times his size.
He showed not the least surprise.
His business wasn't with such.

He gave it scarcely a touch,
And was off on his duty run.
Yet if he encountered one
Of the hive's enquiry squad
Whose work is to find out God
And the nature of time and space,
He would put him onto the case.
Ants are a curious race;
One crossing with hurried tread
The body of one of their dead
Isn't given a moment's arrest—
Seems not even impressed.
But he no doubt reports to any
With whom he crosses antennae,
And they no doubt report
To the higher up at court.
Then word goes forth in Formic:
'Death's come to Jerry McCormic,
Our selfless forager Jerry.
Will the special Janizary
Whose office it is to bury
The dead of the commissary
Go bring him home to his people.
Lay him in state on a sepal.
Wrap him for shroud in a petal.
Embalm him with ichor of nettle.
This is the word of your Queen.'
And presently on the scene
Appears a solemn mortician;
And taking formal position
With feelers calmly atwiddle,
Seizes the dead by the middle,
And heaving him high in air,
Carries him out of there.

No one stands round to stare.
It is nobody else's affair.

It couldn't be called ungentle.
But how thoroughly departmental.

ON THE HEART'S BEGINNING
TO CLOUD THE MIND

Something I saw or thought I saw
In the desert at midnight in Utah,
Looking out of my lower berth
At moonlit sky and moonlit earth.
The sky had here and there a star;
The earth had a single light afar,
A flickering, human pathetic light,
That was maintained against the night,
It seemed to me, by the people there,
With a God-forsaken brute despair.
It would flutter and fall in half an hour
Like the last petal off a flower.
But my heart was beginning to cloud my mind.
I knew a tale of a better kind.
That far light flickers because of trees.
The people can burn it as long as they please:
And when their interests in it end,
They can leave it to someone else to tend.
Come back that way a summer hence,
I should find it no more no less intense.
I pass, but scarcely pass no doubt,
When one will say, 'Let us put it out.'
The other without demur agrees.

They can keep it burning as long as they please;
They can put it out whenever they please.
One looks out last from the darkened room
At the shiny desert with spots of gloom
That might be people and are but cedar,
Have no purpose, have no leader,
Have never made the first move to assemble,
And so are nothing to make her tremble.
She can think of places that are not thus
Without indulging a 'Not for us!'
Life is not so sinister-grave.
Matter of fact has made them brave.
He is husband, she is wife.
She fears not him, they fear not life.
They know where another light has been
And more than one to theirs akin,
But earlier out for bed tonight,
So lost on me in my surface flight.

This I saw when waking late,
Going by at a railroad rate,
Looking through wreaths of engine smoke
Far into the lives of other folk.

AT WOODWARD'S GARDENS

A boy, presuming on his intellect,
Once showed two little monkeys in a cage
A burning-glass they could not understand
And never could be made to understand.
Words are no good: to say it was a lens
For gathering solar rays would not have helped.
But let him show them how the weapon worked.

He made the sun a pin-point on the nose
Of first one, then the other till it brought
A look of puzzled dimness to their eyes
That blinking could not seem to blink away.
They stood arms laced together at the bars,
And exchanged troubled glances over life.
One put a thoughtful hand up to his nose
As if reminded—or as if perhaps
Within a million years of an idea.
He got his purple little knuckles stung.
The already known had once more been confirmed
By psychological experiment,
And that were all the finding to announce
Had the boy not presumed too close and long.
There was a sudden flash of arm, a snatch,
And the glass was the monkeys', not the boy's.
Precipitately they retired back cage
And instituted an investigation
On their part, though without the needed insight.
They bit the glass and listened for the flavor.
They broke the handle and the binding off it.
Then none the wiser, frankly gave it up,
And having hid it in their bedding straw
Against the day of prisoners' ennui,
Came dryly forward to the bars again
To answer for themselves: Who said it mattered
What monkeys did or didn't understand?
They might not understand a burning-glass.
They might not understand the sun itself.
It's knowing what to do with things that counts.

A RECORD STRIDE

In a Vermont bedroom closet
With a door of two broad boards
And for back wall a crumbling old chimney
(And that's what their toes are towards),

I have a pair of shoes standing,
Old rivals of sagging leather,
Who once kept surpassing each other,
But now live even together.

They listen for me in the bedroom
To ask me a thing or two
About who is too old to go walking
With too much stress on the who.

I wet one last year at Montauk
For a hat I had to save.
The other I wet at the Cliff House
In an extra-vagant wave.

Two entirely different grandchildren
Got me into my double adventure.
But when they grow up and can read this
I hope they won't take it for censure.

I touch my tongue to the shoes now
And unless my sense is at fault,
On one I can taste Atlantic,
On the other Pacific, salt.

One foot in each great ocean
Is a record stride or stretch.
The authentic shoes it was made in
I should sell for what they would fetch.

A Record Stride

But instead I proudly devote them
To my museum and muse;
So the thick-skins needn't act thin-skinned
About being past-active shoes.

And I ask all to try to forgive me
For being as over-elated
As if I had measured the country
And got the United States stated.

LOST IN HEAVEN

The clouds, the source of rain, one stormy night
Offered an opening to the source of dew;
Which I accepted with impatient sight,
Looking for my old skymarks in the blue.

But stars were scarce in that part of the sky,
And no two were of the same constellation—
No one was bright enough to identify;
So 'twas with not ungrateful consternation,

Seeing myself well lost once more, I sighed,
'Where, where in Heaven am I? But don't tell me!
Oh, opening clouds, by opening on me wide.
Let's let my heavenly lostness overwhelm me.'

DESERT PLACES

Snow falling and night falling fast, oh, fast
In a field I looked into going past,
And the ground almost covered smooth in snow,
But a few weeds and stubble showing last.

The woods around it have it—it is theirs.
All animals are smothered in their lairs.
I am too absent-spirited to count;
The loneliness includes me unawares.

And lonely as it is that loneliness
Will be more lonely ere it will be less—
A blanker whiteness of benighted snow
With no expression, nothing to express.

They cannot scare me with their empty spaces
Between stars—on stars where no human race is.
I have it in me so much nearer home
To scare myself with my own desert places.

THEY WERE WELCOME
TO THEIR BELIEF

Grief may have thought it was grief.
Care may have thought it was care.
They were welcome to their belief,
The overimportant pair.

No, it took all the snows that clung
To the low roof over his bed,
Beginning when he was young,
To induce the one snow on his head.

But whenever the roof came white
The head in the dark below
Was a shade less the color of night
A shade more the color of snow.

Grief may have thought it was grief.
Care may have thought it was care.
But neither one was the thief
Of his raven color of hair.

THE STRONG ARE SAYING NOTHING

The soil now gets a rumpling soft and damp,
And small regard to the future of any weed.
The final flat of the hoe's approval stamp
Is reserved for the bed of a few selected seed.

There is seldom more than a man to a harrowed piece.
Men work alone, their lots plowed far apart,
One stringing a chain of seed in an open crease,
And another stumbling after a halting cart.

To the fresh and black of the squares of early mold
The leafless bloom of a plum is fresh and white;
Though there's more than a doubt if the weather is not too cold
For the bees to come and serve its beauty aright.

Wind goes from farm to farm in wave on wave,
But carries no cry of what is hoped to be.
There may be little or much beyond the grave,
But the strong are saying nothing until they see.

THE MASTER SPEED

No speed of wind or water rushing by
But you have speed far greater. You can climb
Back up a stream of radiance to the sky,
And back through history up the stream of time.
And you were given this swiftness, not for haste
Nor chiefly that you may go where you will,
But in the rush of everything to waste,
That you may have the power of standing still—
Off any still or moving thing you say.

Two such as you with such a master speed
Cannot be parted nor be swept away
From one another once you are agreed
That life is only life forevermore
Together wing to wing and oar to oar.

NEITHER OUT FAR NOR IN DEEP

The people along the sand
All turn and look one way.
They turn their back on the land.
They look at the sea all day.

As long as it takes to pass
A ship keeps raising its hull;
The wetter ground like glass
Reflects a standing gull.

The land may vary more;
But wherever the truth may be—
The water comes ashore,
And the people look at the sea.

They cannot look out far.
They cannot look in deep.
But when was that ever a bar
To any watch they keep?

VOICE WAYS

Some things are never clear.
But the weather is clear tonight,
Thanks to a clearing rain.

The mountains are brought up near,
The stars are brought out bright.
Your old sweet-cynical strain
Would come in like you here:
'So we won't say nothing is clear.'

DESIGN·

I found a dimpled spider, fat and white,
On a white heal-all, holding up a moth
Like a white piece of rigid satin cloth—
Assorted characters of death and blight
Mixed ready to begin the morning right,
Like the ingredients of a witches' broth—
A snow-drop spider, a flower like a froth,
And dead wings carried like a paper kite.

What had that flower to do with being white,
The wayside blue and innocent heal-all?
What brought the kindred spider to that height,
Then steered the white moth thither in the night?
What but design of darkness to appall?—
If design govern in a thing so small.

ON A BIRD SINGING IN ITS SLEEP

A bird half wakened in the lunar noon
Sang halfway through its little inborn tune.
Partly because it sang but once all night
And that from no especial bush's height;
Partly because it sang ventriloquist
And had the inspiration to desist

Almost before the prick of hostile ears,
It ventured less in peril than appears.
It could not have come down to us so far
Through the interstices of things ajar
On the long bead chain of repeated birth
To be a bird while we are men on earth
If singing out of sleep and dream that way
Had made it much more easily a prey.

UNHARVESTED

A scent of ripeness from over a wall.
And come to leave the routine road
And look for what had made me stall,
There sure enough was an apple tree
That had eased itself of its summer load,
And of all but its trivial foliage free,
Now breathed as light as a lady's fan.
For there there had been an apple fall
As complete as the apple had given man.
The ground was one circle of solid red.

May something go always unharvested!
May much stay out of our stated plan,
Apples or something forgotten and left,
So smelling their sweetness would be no theft.

THERE ARE ROUGHLY ZONES

We sit indoors and talk of the cold outside.
And every gust that gathers strength and heaves
Is a threat to the house. But the house has long been tried.
We think of the tree. If it never again has leaves,

We'll know, we say, that this was the night it died.
It is very far north, we admit, to have brought the peach.
What comes over a man, is it soul or mind—
That to no limits and bounds he can stay confined?
You would say his ambition was to extend the reach
Clear to the Arctic of every living kind.
Why is his nature forever so hard to teach
That though there is no fixed line between wrong and right,
There are roughly zones whose laws must be obeyed.
There is nothing much we can do for the tree tonight,
But we can't help feeling more than a little betrayed
That the northwest wind should rise to such a height
Just when the cold went down so many below.
The tree has no leaves and may never have them again.
We must wait till some months hence in the spring to know.
But if it is destined never again to grow,
It can blame this limitless trait in the hearts of men.

NOT QUITE SOCIAL

Some of you will be glad I did what I did,
And the rest won't want to punish me too severely
For finding a thing to do that though not forbid
Yet wasn't enjoined and wasn't expected clearly.

To punish me overcruelly wouldn't be right
For merely giving you once more gentle proof
That the city's hold on a man is no more tight
Than when its walls rose higher than any roof.

You may taunt me with not being able to flee the earth.
You have me there, but loosely as I would be held.
The way of understanding is partly mirth.
I would not be taken as ever having rebelled.

And anyone is free to condemn me to death—
If he leaves it to nature to carry out the sentence.
I shall will to the common stock of air my breath
And pay a death-tax of fairly polite repentance.

PROVIDE, PROVIDE

The witch that came (the withered hag)
To wash the steps with pail and rag,
Was once the beauty Abishag,

The picture pride of Hollywood.
Too many fall from great and good
For you to doubt the likelihood.

Die early and avoid the fate.
Or if predestined to die late,
Make up your mind to die in state.

Make the whole stock exchange your own!
If need be occupy a throne,
Where nobody can call *you* crone.

Some have relied on what they knew;
Others on being simply true.
What worked for them might work for you.

No memory of having starred
Atones for later disregard,
Or keeps the end from being hard.

Better to go down dignified
With boughten friendship at your side
Than none at all. Provide, provide!

TEN MILLS

PRECAUTION

I never dared be radical when young
For fear it would make me conservative when old.

THE SPAN OF LIFE

The old dog barks backward without getting up.
I can remember when he was a pup.

THE WRIGHTS' BIPLANE

This biplane is the shape of human flight.
Its name might better be First Motor Kite.
Its makers' name—Time cannot get that wrong,
For it was writ in heaven doubly Wright.

EVIL TENDENCIES CANCEL

Will the blight end the chestnut?
The farmers rather guess not.
It keeps smoldering at the roots
And sending up new shoots
Till another parasite
Shall come to end the blight.

PERTINAX

Let chaos storm!
Let cloud shapes swarm!
I wait for form.

WASPISH

On glossy wires artistically bent,
He draws himself up to his full extent.
His natty wings with self-assurance perk.
His stinging quarters menacingly work.
Poor egotist, he has no way of knowing
But he's as good as anybody going.

ONE GUESS

He has dust in his eyes and a fan for a wing,
A leg akimbo with which he can sing,
And a mouthful of dye stuff instead of a sting.

THE HARDSHIP OF ACCOUNTING

Never ask of money spent
Where the spender thinks it went.
Nobody was ever meant
To remember or invent
What he did with every cent.

NOT ALL THERE

I turned to speak to God
About the world's despair;
But to make bad matters worse
I found God wasn't there.

God turned to speak to me
(Don't anybody laugh)
God found I wasn't there—
At least not over half.

IN DIVÉS' DIVE

It is late at night and still I am losing,
But still I am steady and unaccusing.

As long as the Declaration guards
My right to be equal in number of cards,

It is nothing to me who runs the Dive.
Let's have a look at another five.

THE VINDICTIVES

You like to hear about gold.
A king filled his prison room
As full as the room could hold
To the top of his reach on the wall
With every known shape of the stuff.
'Twas to buy himself off his doom.
But it wasn't ransom enough.
His captors accepted it all,
But didn't let go of the king.
They made him send out a call
To his subjects to gather them more.
And his subjects wrung all they could **wring**
Out of temple and palace and store.
But when there seemed no more to bring,
His captors convicted the king
Of once having started a war,
And strangled the wretch with a string.

But really that gold was not half
That a king might have hoped to compel—
Not a half, not a third, not a tithe.
The king had scarce ceased to writhe,
When hate gave a terrible laugh,
Like a manhole opened to Hell.
If gold pleased the conqueror, well,
That gold should be the one thing
The conqueror henceforth should lack.

They gave no more thought to the king.
All joined in the game of hide-gold.

They swore all the gold should go back
Deep into the earth whence it came.

Their minds ran on cranny and crack.
All joined in the maddening game.
The tale is still boastingly told
Of many a treasure by name
That vanished into the black
And put out its light for the foe.

That self-sack and self-overthrow,
That was the splendidest sack
Since the forest Germans sacked Rome
And took the gold candlesticks home.

One Inca prince on the rack,
And late in his last hour alive,
Told them in what lake to dive
To seek what they seemed so to want.
They dived and nothing was found.
He told them to dive till they drowned.
The whole fierce conquering pack
Hunted and tortured and raged.
There were suns of story and vaunt
They searched for into Brazil
Their tongues hanging out unassuaged.

But the conquered grew meek and still.
They slowly and silently aged.
They kept their secrets and died,
Maliciously satisfied.
One knew of a burial hole
In the floor of a tribal cave,
Where under deep ash and charcoal

And cracked bones, human and beast,
The midden of feast upon feast,
Was coiled in its last resting grave
The great treasure wanted the most,
The great thousand-linked gold chain,
Each link of a hundredweight,
That once between post and post
(In-leaning under the strain),
And looped ten times back and forth,
Had served as a palace gate.
Some said it had gone to the coast,
Some over the mountains east,
Some into the country north,
On the backs of a single-file host,
Commanded by one sun-priest,
And raising a dust with a train
Of flashing links in the sun.
No matter what some may say.
(The saying is never done.)
There bright in the filth it lay
Untarnished by rust and decay.
And be all plunderers curst.

'The best way to hate is the worst.
'Tis to find what the hated need,
Never mind of what actual worth,
And wipe that out of the earth.
Let them die of unsatisfied greed,
Of unsatisfied love of display,
Of unsatisfied love of the high,
Unvulgar, unsoiled, and ideal.
Let their trappings be taken away.
Let them suffer starvation and die
Of being brought down to the real.'

IRIS BY NIGHT

One misty evening, one another's guide,
We two were groping down a Malvern side
The last wet fields and dripping hedges home.
There came a moment of confusing lights,
Such as according to belief in Rome
Were seen of old at Memphis on the heights
Before the fragments of a former sun
Could concentrate anew and rise as one.
Light was a paste of pigment in our eyes.
And then there was a moon and then a scene
So watery as to seem submarine;
In which we two stood saturated, drowned.
The clover-mingled rowan on the ground
Had taken all the water it could as dew,
And still the air was saturated too,
Its airy pressure turned to water weight.
Then a small rainbow like a trellis gate,
A very small moon-made prismatic bow,
Stood closely over us through which to go.
And then we were vouchsafed the miracle
That never yet to other two befell
And I alone of us have lived to tell.
A wonder! Bow and rainbow as it bent,
Instead of moving with us as we went,
(To keep the pots of gold from being found)
It lifted from its dewy pediment
Its two mote-swimming many-colored ends,
And gathered them together in a ring.
And we stood in it softly circled round
From all division time or foe can bring
In a relation of elected friends.

BUILD SOIL—A POLITICAL PASTORAL

Why, Tityrus! But you've forgotten me.
I'm Meliboeus the potato man,
The one you had the talk with, you remember,
Here on this very campus years ago.
Hard times have struck me and I'm on the move.
I've had to give my interval farm up
For interest, and I've bought a mountain farm
For nothing down, all-out-doors of a place,
All woods and pasture only fit for sheep.
But sheep is what I'm going into next.
I'm done forever with potato crops
At thirty cents a bushel. Give me sheep.
I know wool's down to seven cents a pound.
But I don't calculate to sell my wool.
I didn't my potatoes. I consumed them.
I'll dress up in sheep's clothing and eat sheep.
The Muse takes care of you. You live by writing
Your poems on a farm and call that farming.
Oh, I don't blame you. I say take life easy.
I should myself, only I don't know how.
But have some pity on us who have to work.
Why don't you use your talents as a writer
To advertise our farms to city buyers,
Or else write something to improve food prices.
Get in a poem toward the next election.

Oh, Meliboeus, I have half a mind
To take a writing hand in politics.

Before now poetry has taken notice
Of wars, and what are wars but politics
Transformed from chronic to acute and bloody?

I may be wrong, but, Tityrus, to me
The times seem revolutionary bad.

The question is whether they've reached a depth
Of desperation that would warrant poetry's
Leaving love's alternations, joy and grief,
The weather's alternations, summer and winter,
Our age-long theme, for the uncertainty
Of judging who is a contemporary liar—
Who in particular, when all alike
Get called as much in clashes of ambition.
Life may be tragically bad, and I
Make bold to sing it so, but do I dare
Name names and tell you who by name is wicked?
Whittier's luck with Skipper Ireson awes me.
Many men's luck with Greatest Washington
(Who sat for Stuart's portrait, but who sat
Equally for the nation's Constitution).
I prefer to sing safely in the realm
Of types, composite and imagined people:
To affirm there is such a thing as evil
Personified, but ask to be excused
From saying on a jury 'Here's the guilty.'

I doubt if you're convinced the times are bad.
I keep my eye on Congress, Meliboeus.
They're in the best position of us all
To know if anything is very wrong.
I mean they could be trusted to give the alarm
If earth were thought about to change its axis,

Or a star coming to dilate the sun.
As long as lightly all their live-long sessions,
Like a yard full of school boys out at recess
Before their plays and games were organized,
They yelling mix tag, hide-and-seek, hop-scotch,
And leap frog in each other's way,—all's well.
Let newspapers profess to fear the worst!
Nothing's portentous, I am reassured.

Is socialism needed, do you think?

We have it now. For socialism is
An element in any government.
There's no such thing as socialism pure—
Except as an abstraction of the mind.
There's only democratic socialism
Monarchic socialism—oligarchic,
The last being what they seem to have in Russia.
You often get it most in monarchy,
Least in democracy. In practice, pure,
I don't know what it would be. No one knows.
I have no doubt like all the loves when
Philosophized together into one—
One sickness of the body and the soul.
Thank God our practice holds the loves apart
Beyond embarrassing self-consciousness
Where natural friends are met, where dogs are kept,
Where women pray with priests. There is no love.
There's only love of men and women, love
Of children, love of friends, of men, of God,
Divine love, human love, parental love,
Roughly discriminated for the rough.

Poetry, itself once more, is back in love.

Pardon the analogy, my Meliboeus,
For sweeping me away. Let's see, where was I?

But don't you think more should be socialized
Than is?

What should you mean by socialized?

Made good for everyone—things like inventions—
Made so we all should get the good of them—
All, not just great exploiting businesses.

We sometimes only get the bad of them.
In your sense of the word ambition has
Been socialized—the first propensity
To be attempted. Greed may well come next.
But the worst one of all to leave uncurbed,
Unsocialized, is ingenuity:
Which for no sordid self-aggrandizement,
For nothing but its own blind satisfaction
(In this it is as much like hate as love)
Works in the dark as much against as for us.
Even while we talk some chemist at Columbia
Is stealthily contriving wool from jute
That when let loose upon the grazing world
Will put ten thousand farmers out of sheep.
Everyone asks for freedom for himself,
The man free love, the business man free trade,
The writer and talker free speech and free press.
Political ambition has been taught,
By being punished back, it is not free:
It must at some point gracefully refrain.

Greed has been taught a little abnegation
And shall be more before we're done with it.
It is just fool enough to think itself
Self-taught. But our brute snarling and lashing taught it.
None shall be as ambitious as he can.
None should be as ingenious as he could,
Not if I had my say. Bounds should be set
To ingenuity for being so cruel
In bringing change unheralded on the unready.

I elect you to put the curb on it.

Were I dictator, I'll tell you what I'd do.

What should you do?

                    I'd let things take their course
And then I'd claim the credit for the outcome.

You'd make a sort of safety-first dictator.

Don't let the things I say against myself
Betray you into taking sides against me,
Or it might get you into trouble with me.
I'm not afraid to prophesy the future,
And be judged by the outcome, Meliboeus.
Listen and I will take my dearest risk.
We're always too much out or too much in.
At present from a cosmical dilation
We're so much out that the odds are against
Our ever getting inside in again.
But inside in is where we've got to get.
My friends all know I'm interpersonal.

But long before I'm interpersonal
Away 'way down inside I'm personal.
Just so before we're international
We're national and act as nationals.
The colors are kept unmixed on the palette,
Or better on dish plates all around the room,
So the effect when they are mixed on canvas
May seem almost exclusively designed.
Some minds are so confounded intermental
They remind me of pictures on a palette:
'Look at what happened. Surely some God pinxit.
Come look at my significant mud pie.'
It's hard to tell which is the worse abhorrence
Whether it's persons pied or nations pied.
Don't let me seem to say the exchange, the encounter,
May not be the important thing at last.
It well may be. We meet—I don't say when—
But must bring to the meeting the maturest,
The longest-saved-up, raciest, localest
We have strength of reserve in us to bring.

Tityrus, sometimes I'm perplexed myself
To find the good of commerce. Why should I
Have to sell you my apples and buy yours?
It can't be just to give the robber a chance
To catch them and take toll of them in transit.
Too mean a thought to get much comfort out of.
I figure that like any bandying
Of words or toys, it ministers to health.
It very likely quickens and refines us.

To market 'tis our destiny to go.
But much as in the end we bring for sale there
There is still more we never bring or should bring;

More that should be kept back—the soil for instance
In my opinion,—though we both know poets
Who fall all over each other to bring soil
And even subsoil and hardpan to market.
To sell the hay off, let alone the soil,
Is an unpardonable sin in farming.
The moral is, make a late start to market.
Let me preach to you, will you, Meliboeus?

Preach on. I thought you were already preaching.
But preach and see if I can tell the difference.

Needless to say to you, my argument
Is not to lure the city to the country.
Let those possess the land and only those,
Who love it with a love so strong and stupid
That they may be abused and taken advantage of
And made fun of by business, law, and art;
They still hang on. That so much of the earth's
Unoccupied need not make us uneasy.
We don't pretend to complete occupancy.
The world's one globe, human society
Another softer globe that slightly flattened
Rests on the world, and clinging slowly rolls.
We have our own round shape to keep unbroken.
The world's size has no more to do with us
Than has the universe's. We are balls,
We are round from the same source of roundness.
We are both round because the mind is round,
Because all reasoning is in a circle.
At least that's why the universe is round.

If what you're preaching is a line of conduct,
Just what am I supposed to do about it?
Reason in circles?

No, refuse to be
Seduced back to the land by any claim
The land may seem to have on man to use it.
Let none assume to till the land but farmers.
I only speak to you as one of them.
You shall go to your run-out mountain farm,
Poor castaway of commerce, and so live
That none shall ever see you come to market—
Not for a long long time. Plant, breed, produce,
But what you raise or grow, why feed it out,
Eat it or plow it under where it stands
To build the soil. For what is more accursed
Than an impoverished soil pale and metallic?
What cries more to our kind for sympathy?
I'll make a compact with you, Meliboeus,
To match you deed for deed and plan for plan.
Friends crowd around me with their five-year plans
That Soviet Russia has made fashionable.
You come to me and I'll unfold to you
A five-year plan I call so, not because
It takes ten years or so to carry out,
Rather because it took five years at least
To think it out. Come close, let us conspire—
In self-restraint, if in restraint of trade.
You will go to your run-out mountain farm
And do what I command you. I take care
To command only what you meant to do
Anyway. That is my style of dictator.
Build soil. Turn the farm in upon itself
Until it can contain itself no more,
But sweating-full, drips wine and oil a little.
I will go to my run-out social mind
And be as unsocial with it as I can.
The thought I have, and my first impulse is

To take to market—I will turn it under.
The thought from that thought—I will turn it under
And so on to the limit of my nature.
We are too much out, and if we won't draw in
We shall be driven in. I was brought up,
A state-rights free-trade Democrat. What's that?
An inconsistency. The state shall be
Laws to itself, it seems, and yet have no
Control of what it sells or what it buys.
Suppose someone comes near me who in rate
Of speech and thinking is so much my better
I am imposed on, silenced and discouraged.
Do I submit to being supplied by him
As the more economical producer,
More wonderful, more beautiful producer?
No. I unostentatiously move off
Far enough for my thought-flow to resume.
Thought product and food product are to me
Nothing compared to the producing of them.
I sent you once a song with the refrain:

        Let me be the one
        To do what is done—

My share at least lest I be empty-idle.
Keep off each other and keep each other off.
You see the beauty of my proposal is
It needn't wait on general revolution.
I bid you to a one-man revolution—
The only revolution that is coming.
We're too unseparate out among each other—
With goods to sell and notions to impart.
A youngster comes to me with half a quatrain
To ask me if I think it worth the pains

Of working out the rest, the other half.
I am brought guaranteed young prattle poems
Made publicly in school, above suspicion
Of plagiarism and help of cheating parents.
We congregate embracing from distrust
As much as love, and too close in to strike
And be so very striking. Steal away
The song says. Steal away and stay away.
Don't join too many gangs. Join few if any.
Join the United States and join the family—
But not much in between unless a college.
Is it a bargain, Shepherd Meliboeus?

Probably, but you're far too fast and strong
For my mind to keep working in your presence.
I can tell better after I get home,
Better a month from now when cutting posts
Or mending fence it all comes back to me
What I was thinking when you interrupted
My life-train logic. I agree with you
We're too unseparate. And going home
From company means coming to our senses.

A Witness Tree

BEECH

Where my imaginary line
Bends square in woods, an iron spine
And pile of real rocks have been founded.
And off this corner in the wild,
Where these are driven in and piled,
One tree, by being deeply wounded,
Has been impressed as Witness Tree
And made commit to memory
My proof of being not unbounded.
Thus truth's established and borne out,
Though circumstanced with dark and doubt—
Though by a world of doubt surrounded.

The Moodie Forester

SYCAMORE

Zaccheus he
Did climb the tree
Our Lord to see.

The New England Primer

THE SILKEN TENT

[handwritten margin note: description of a woman]

[handwritten margin note: freedom depends upon control]

She is as in a field a silken tent
At midday when a sunny summer breeze
Has dried the dew and all its ropes relent,
So that in guys it gently sways at ease,
And its supporting central cedar pole, *[handwritten margin note: religion main support for relationship with a man]*
That is its pinnacle to heavenward
And signifies the sureness of the soul,
Seems to owe naught to any single cord,
But strictly held by none, is loosely bound
By countless silken ties of love and thought
To everything on earth the compass round,
And only by one's going slightly taut
In the capriciousness of summer air
Is of the slightest bondage made aware.

ALL REVELATION

A head thrusts in as for the view,
But where it is it thrusts in from
Or what it is it thrusts into
By that Cyb'laean avenue,
And what can of its coming come,

And whither it will be withdrawn,
And what take hence or leave behind,
These things the mind has pondered on
A moment and still asking gone.
Strange apparition of the mind!

But the impervious geode
Was entered, and its inner crust
Of crystals with a ray cathode
At every point and facet glowed
In answer to the mental thrust.

Eyes seeking the response of eyes
Bring out the stars, bring out the flowers,
Thus concentrating earth and skies
So none need be afraid of size.
All revelation has been ours.

HAPPINESS MAKES UP IN HEIGHT
FOR WHAT IT LACKS IN LENGTH

Oh, stormy stormy world,
The days you were not swirled
Around with mist and cloud,
Or wrapped as in a shroud,
And the sun's brilliant ball
Was not in part or all
Obscured from mortal view—
Were days so very few
I can but wonder whence
I get the lasting sense
Of so much warmth and light.
If my mistrust is right
It may be altogether
From one day's perfect weather,
When starting clear at dawn,
The day swept clearly on
To finish clear at eve.
I verily believe

A Witness Tree

My fair impression may
Be all from that one day
No shadow crossed but ours
As through its blazing flowers
We went from house to wood
For change of solitude.

COME IN

As I came to the edge of the woods,
Thrush music—hark!
Now if it was dusk outside,
Inside it was dark.

Too dark in the woods for a bird
By sleight of wing
To better its perch for the night,
Though it still could sing.

The last of the light of the sun
That had died in the west
Still lived for one song more
In a thrush's breast.

Far in the pillared dark
Thrush music went—
Almost like a call to come in
To the dark and lament.

But no, I was out for stars:
I would not come in.
I meant not even if asked,
And I hadn't been.

[handwritten marginalia:] the world is made for us—not true

[handwritten marginalia:] religious experience vs scientific experience

[handwritten marginalia:] man striving for the absolute

[handwritten marginalia:] idea of space

I COULD GIVE ALL TO TIME

To Time it never seems that he is brave
To set himself against the peaks of snow
To lay them level with the running wave,
Nor is he overjoyed when they lie low,
But only grave, contemplative and grave.

What now is inland shall be ocean isle,
Then eddies playing round a sunken reef
Like the curl at the corner of a smile;
And I could share Time's lack of joy or grief
At such a planetary change of style.

I could give all to Time except—except
What I myself have held. But why declare
The things forbidden that while the Customs slept
I have crossed to Safety with? For I am There,
And what I would not part with I have kept.

CARPE DIEM

Age saw two quiet children
Go loving by at twilight,
He knew not whether homeward,
Or outward from the village,
Or (chimes were ringing) churchward.
He waited (they were strangers)
Till they were out of hearing
To bid them both be happy.
'Be happy, happy, happy,
And seize the day of pleasure.'
The age-long theme is Age's.

223

'Twas Age imposed on poems
Their gather-roses burden
To warn against the danger
That overtaken lovers
From being overflooded
With happiness should have it
And yet not know they have it.
But bid life seize the present?
It lives less in the present
Than in the future always,
And less in both together
Than in the past. The present
Is too much for the senses,
Too crowding, too confusing—
Too present to imagine.

THE MOST OF IT

He thought he kept the universe alone;
For all the voice in answer he could wake
Was but the mocking echo of his own
From some tree-hidden cliff across the lake.
Some morning from the boulder-broken beach
He would cry out on life, that what it wants
Is not its own love back in copy speech,
But counter-love, original response.
And nothing ever came of what he cried
Unless it was the embodiment that crashed
In the cliff's talus on the other side,
And then in the far distant water splashed,
But after a time allowed for it to swim,
Instead of proving human when it neared
And someone else additional to him,

As a great buck it powerfully appeared,
Pushing the crumpled water up ahead,
And landed pouring like a waterfall,
And stumbled through the rocks with horny tread,
And forced the underbrush—and that was all.

NEVER AGAIN WOULD BIRDS' SONG
BE THE SAME

He would declare and could himself believe
That the birds there in all the garden round
From having heard the daylong voice of Eve
Had added to their own an oversound,
Her tone of meaning but without the words.
Admittedly an eloquence so soft
Could only have had an influence on birds
When call or laughter carried it aloft.
Be that as may be, she was in their song.
Moreover her voice upon their voices crossed
Had now persisted in the woods so long
That probably it never would be lost.
Never again would birds' song be the same.
And to do that to birds was why she came.

THE SUBVERTED FLOWER

She drew back; he was calm:
'It is this that had the power.'
And he lashed his open palm
With the tender-headed flower.
He smiled for her to smile,
But she was either blind

Or willfully unkind.
He eyed her for a while
For a woman and a puzzle.
He flicked and flung the flower,
And another sort of smile
Caught up like finger tips
The corners of his lips
And cracked his ragged muzzle.
She was standing to the waist
In goldenrod and brake,
Her shining hair displaced.
He stretched her either arm
As if she made it ache
To clasp her—not to harm;
As if he could not spare
To touch her neck and hair.
'If this has come to us
And not to me alone—'
So she thought she heard him say;
Though with every word he spoke
His lips were sucked and blown
And the effort made him choke
Like a tiger at a bone.
She had to lean away.
She dared not stir a foot,
Lest movement should provoke
The demon of pursuit
That slumbers in a brute.
It was then her mother's call
From inside the garden wall
Made her steal a look of fear
To see if he could hear
And would pounce to end it all
Before her mother came.

The Subverted Flower

She looked and saw the shame:
A hand hung like a paw,
An arm worked like a saw
As if to be persuasive,
An ingratiating laugh
That cut the snout in half,
An eye become evasive.
A girl could only see
That a flower had marred a man,
But what she could not see
Was that the flower might be
Other than base and fetid:
That the flower had done but part,
And what the flower began
Her own too meager heart
Had terribly completed.
She looked and saw the worst.
And the dog or what it was,
Obeying bestial laws,
A coward save at night,
Turned from the place and ran.
She heard him stumble first
And use his hands in flight.
She heard him bark outright.
And oh, for one so young
The bitter words she spit
Like some tenacious bit
That will not leave the tongue.
She plucked her lips for it,
And still the horror clung.
Her mother wiped the foam
From her chin, picked up her comb
And drew her backward home.

WILLFUL HOMING

It is getting dark and time he drew to a house,
But the blizzard blinds him to any house ahead.
The storm gets down his neck in an icy souse
That sucks his breath like a wicked cat in bed.

The snow blows on him and off him, exerting force
Downward to make him sit astride a drift,
Imprint a saddle and calmly consider a course.
He peers out shrewdly into the thick and swift.

Since he means to come to a door he will come to a door,
Although so compromised of aim and rate
He may fumble wide of the knob a yard or more,
And to those concerned he may seem a little late.

A CLOUD SHADOW

A breeze discovered my open book
And began to flutter the leaves to look
For a poem there used to be on Spring.
I tried to tell her 'There's no such thing!'

For whom would a poem on Spring be by?
The breeze disdained to make reply;
And a cloud shadow crossed her face
For fear I would make her miss the place.

THE QUEST OF THE PURPLE-FRINGED

I felt the chill of the meadow underfoot,
But the sun overhead;
And snatches of verse and song of scenes like this
I sung or said.

I skirted the margin alders for miles and miles
In a sweeping line.
The day was the day by every flower that blooms,
But I saw no sign.

Yet further I went to be before the scythe,
For the grass was high;
Till I saw the path where the slender fox had come
And gone panting by.

Then at last and following him I found—
In the very hour
When the color flushed to the petals it must have been—
The far-sought flower.

There stood the purple spires with no breath of air
Nor headlong bee
To disturb their perfect poise the livelong day
'Neath the alder tree.

I only knelt and putting the boughs aside
Looked, or at most
Counted them all to the buds in the copse's depth
That were pale as a ghost.

Then I arose and silently wandered home,
And I for one
Said that the fall might come and whirl of leaves,
For summer was done.

TRIPLE BRONZE

The Infinite's being so wide
Is the reason the Powers provide
For inner defense my hide.
For next defense outside

I make myself this time
Of wood or granite or lime
A wall too hard for crime
Either to breach or climb.

Then a number of us agree
On a national boundary.
And that defense makes three
Between too much and me.

OUR HOLD ON THE PLANET

We asked for rain. It didn't flash and roar.
It didn't lose its temper at our demand.
And blow a gale. It didn't misunderstand
And give us more than our spokesman bargained for;
And just because we owned to a wish for rain,
Send us a flood and bid us be damned and drown.
It gently threw us a glittering shower down.
And when we had taken that into the roots of grain,
It threw us another and then another still
Till the spongy soil again was natal wet.

We may doubt the just proportion of good to ill.
There is much in nature against us. But we forget:
Take nature altogether since time began,
Including human nature, in peace and war,
And it must be a little more in favor of man,
Say a fraction of one per cent at the very least,
Or our number living wouldn't be steadily more,
Our hold on the planet wouldn't have so increased.

TO A YOUNG WRETCH

(*Boethian*)

As gay for you to take your father's ax
As take his gun—rod—to go hunting—fishing.
You nick my spruce until its fiber cracks,
It gives up standing straight and goes down swishing.
You link an arm in its arm and you lean
Across the light snow homeward smelling green.

I could have bought you just as good a tree
To frizzle resin in a candle flame,
And what a saving 'twould have meant to me.
But tree by charity is not the same
As tree by enterprise and expedition.
I must not spoil your Christmas with contrition.

It is your Christmases against my woods.
But even where thus opposing interests kill,
They are to be thought of as opposing goods
Oftener than as conflicting good and ill;
Which makes the war god seem no special dunce
For always fighting on both sides at once.

And though in tinsel chain and popcorn rope,
My tree a captive in your window bay
Has lost its footing on my mountain slope
And lost the stars of heaven, may, oh, may
The symbol star it lifts against your ceiling
Help me accept its fate with Christmas feeling.

THE LESSON FOR TODAY *

If this uncertain age in which we dwell
Were really as dark as I hear sages tell,
And I convinced that they were really sages,
I should not curse myself with it to hell,
But leaving not the chair I long have sat in,
I should betake me back ten thousand pages
To the world's undebatably dark ages,
And getting up my medieval Latin,
Seek converse common cause and brotherhood
(By all that's liberal—I should, I should)
With poets who could calmly take the fate
Of being born at once too early and late,
And for these reasons kept from being great.
Yet singing but Dione in the wood
And *ver aspergit terram floribus*
They slowly led old Latin verse to rhyme
And to forget the ancient lengths of time,
And so began the modern world for us.

I'd say, O Master of the Palace School,
You were not Charles' nor anybody's fool:

---

* Read before the Phi Beta Kappa Society at Harvard University, June 20, 1941.

The Lesson for Today

Tell me as pedagogue to pedagogue,
You did not know that since King Charles did rule
You had no chance but to be minor, did you?
Your light was spent perhaps as in a fog
That at once kept you burning low and hid you.
The age may very well have been to blame
For your not having won to Virgil's fame.
But no one ever heard you make the claim.
You would not think you knew enough to judge
The age when full upon you. That's my point.
We have today and I could call their name
Who know exactly what is out of joint
To make their verse and their excuses lame.
They've tried to grasp with too much social fact
Too large a situation. You and I
Would be afraid if we should comprehend
And get outside of too much bad statistics
Our muscles never could again contract:
We never could recover human shape,
But must live lives out mentally agape,
Or die of philosophical distention.
That's how we feel—and we're no special mystics.

  We can't appraise the time in which we act.
But for the folly of it, let's pretend
We know enough to know it for adverse.
One more millennium's about to end.
Let's celebrate the event, my distant friend,
In publicly disputing which is worse,
The present age or your age. You and I
As schoolmen of repute should qualify
To wage a fine scholastical contention
As to whose age deserves the lower mark,
Or should I say the higher one, for dark.

I can just hear the way you make it go:
There's always something to be sorry for,
A sordid peace or an outrageous war.
Yes, yes, of course. We have the same convention.
The groundwork of all faith is human woe.
It was well worth preliminary mention.
There's nothing but injustice to be had,
No choice is left a poet, you might add,
But how to take the curse, tragic or comic.
It was well worth preliminary mention.
But let's go on to where our cases part,
If part they do. Let me propose a start.
(We're rivals in the badness of our case,
Remember, and must keep a solemn face.)
Space ails us moderns: we are sick with space.
Its contemplation makes us out as small
As a brief epidemic of microbes
That in a good glass may be seen to crawl
The patina of this the least of globes.
But have we there the advantage after all?
You were belittled into vilest worms
God hardly tolerated with his feet;
Which comes to the same thing in different terms.
We both are the belittled human race,
One as compared with God and one with space.
I had thought ours the more profound disgrace;
But doubtless this was only my conceit.
The cloister and the observatory saint
Take comfort in about the same complaint.
So science and religion really meet.

I can just hear you call your Palace class:
Come learn the Latin Eheu for alas.
You may not want to use it and you may.

The Lesson for Today

O paladins, the lesson for today
Is how to be unhappy yet polite.
And at the summons Roland, Olivier,
And every sheepish paladin and peer,
Being already more than proved in fight,
Sits down in school to try if he can write
Like Horace in the true Horatian vein,
Yet like a Christian disciplined to bend
His mind to thinking always of the end.
Memento mori and obey the Lord.
Art and religion love the somber chord.
Earth's a hard place in which to save the soul,
And could it be brought under state control,
So automatically we all were saved,
Its separateness from Heaven could be waived;
It might as well at once be kingdom-come.
(Perhaps it will be next millennium.)

But these are universals, not confined
To any one time, place, or human kind.
We're either nothing or a God's regret.
As ever when philosophers are met,
No matter where they stoutly mean to get,
Nor what particulars they reason from,
They are philosophers, and from old habit
They end up in the universal Whole
As unoriginal as any rabbit.

One age is like another for the soul.
I'm telling you. You haven't said a thing,
Unless I put it in your mouth to say.
I'm having the whole argument my way—
But in your favor—please to tell your King—
In having granted you all ages shine

With equal darkness, yours as dark as mine.
I'm liberal. You, you aristocrat,
Won't know exactly what I mean by that.
I mean so altruistically moral
I never take my own side in a quarrel.
I'd lay my hand on his hand on his staff,
Lean back and have my confidential laugh,
And tell him I had read his Epitaph.

It sent me to the graves the other day.
The only other there was far away
Across the landscape with a watering pot
At his devotions in a special plot.
And he was there resuscitating flowers
(Make no mistake about its being bones);
But I was only there to read the stones
To see what on the whole they had to say
About how long a man may think to live,
Which is becoming my concern of late.
And very wide the choice they seemed to give;
The ages ranging all the way from hours
To months and years and many many years.
One man had lived one hundred years and eight.
But though we all may be inclined to wait
And follow some development of state,
Or see what comes of science and invention,
There is a limit to our time extension.
We all are doomed to broken-off careers,
And so's the nation, so's the total race.
The earth itself is liable to the fate
Of meaninglessly being broken off.
(And hence so many literary tears
At which my inclination is to scoff.)
I may have wept that any should have died

Or missed their chance, or not have been their best,
Or been their riches, fame, or love denied;
On me as much as any is the jest.
I take my incompleteness with the rest.
God bless himself can no one else be blessed.

   I hold your doctrine of Memento Mori.
And were an epitaph to be my story
I'd have a short one ready for my own.
I would have written of me on my stone:
I had a lover's quarrel with the world.

TIME OUT *

It took that pause to make him realize
The mountain he was climbing had the slant
As of a book held up before his eyes
(And was a text albeit done in plant).
Dwarf cornel, gold-thread, and maianthemum,
He followingly fingered as he read,
The flowers fading on the seed to come;
But the thing was the slope it gave his head:
The same for reading as it was for thought,
So different from the hard and level stare
Of enemies defied and battles fought.
It was the obstinately gentle air
That may be clamored at by cause and sect
But it will have its moment to reflect.

TO A MOTH SEEN IN WINTER

Here's first a gloveless hand warm from my pocket,
A perch and resting place 'twixt wood and wood,
Bright-black-eyed silvery creature, brushed with brown,
The wings not folded in repose, but spread.
(Who would you be, I wonder, by those marks
If I had moths to friend as I have flowers?)
And now pray tell what lured you with false hope

---

* Read before the Phi Beta Kappa Society at William and Mary
College, December 5, 1941.

To make the venture of eternity
And seek the love of kind in wintertime?
But stay and hear me out. I surely think
You make a labor of flight for one so airy,
Spending yourself too much in self-support.
Nor will you find love either nor love you.
And what I pity in you is something human,
The old incurable untimeliness,
Only begetter of all ills that are.
But go. You are right. My pity cannot help.
Go till you wet your pinions and are quenched.
You must be made more simply wise than I
To know the hand I stretch impulsively
Across the gulf of well nigh everything
May reach to you, but cannot touch your fate.
I cannot touch your life, much less can save,
Who am tasked to save my own a little while.

Circa 1900

A CONSIDERABLE SPECK

(Microscopic)

A speck that would have been beneath my sight
On any but a paper sheet so white
Set off across what I had written there.
And I had idly poised my pen in air
To stop it with a period of ink
When something strange about it made me think.
This was no dust speck by my breathing blown,
But unmistakably a living mite
With inclinations it could call its own.

It paused as with suspicion of my pen,
And then came racing wildly on again
To where my manuscript was not yet dry;
Then paused again and either drank or smelt—
With loathing, for again it turned to fly.
Plainly with an intelligence I dealt.
It seemed too tiny to have room for feet,
Yet must have had a set of them complete
To express how much it didn't want to die.
It ran with terror and with cunning crept.
It faltered: I could see it hesitate;
Then in the middle of the open sheet
Cower down in desperation to accept
Whatever I accorded it of fate.
I have none of the tenderer-than-thou
Collectivistic regimenting love
With which the modern world is being swept.
But this poor microscopic item now!
Since it was nothing I knew evil of
I let it lie there till I hope it slept.

I have a mind myself and recognize
Mind when I meet with it in any guise.
No one can know how glad I am to find
On any sheet the least display of mind.

THE LOST FOLLOWER

As I have known them passionate and fine
The gold for which they leave the golden line
Of lyric is a golden light divine,
Never the gold of darkness from a mine.

The Lost Follower

The spirit plays us strange religious pranks
To whatsoever god we owe the thanks.
No one has ever failed the poet ranks
To link a chain of money-metal banks.

The loss to song, the danger of defection
Is always in the opposite direction.
Some turn in sheer, in Shelleyan dejection
To try if one more popular election

Will give us by short cut the final stage
That poetry with all its golden rage
For beauty on the illuminated page
Has failed to bring—I mean the Golden Age.

And if this may not be (and nothing's sure),
At least to live ungolden with the poor,
Enduring what the ungolden must endure.
This has been poetry's great anti-lure.

The muse mourns one who went to his retreat
Long since in some abysmal city street,
The bride who shared the crust he broke to eat
As grave as he about the world's defeat.

With such it has proved dangerous as friend
Even in a playful moment to contend
That the millennium to which you bend
In longing is not at a progress-end

By grace of state-manipulated pelf,
Or politics of Ghibelline or Guelph,
But right beside you book-like on a shelf,
Or even better god-like in yourself.

He trusts my love too well to deign reply.
But there is in the sadness of his eye,
Something about a kingdom in the sky
(As yet unbrought to earth) he means to try.

NOVEMBER

We saw leaves go to glory,
Then almost migratory
Go part way down the lane,
And then to end the story
Get beaten down and pasted
In one wild day of rain.
We heard ' 'Tis over' roaring.
A year of leaves was wasted.
Oh, we make a boast of storing,
Of saving and of keeping,
But only by ignoring
The waste of moments sleeping,
The waste of pleasure weeping,
By denying and ignoring
The waste of nations warring.

1938

THE RABBIT HUNTER

Careless and still
The hunter lurks
With gun depressed,
Facing alone
The alder swamps
Ghastly snow-white.

And his hound works
In the offing there
Like one possessed,
And yelps delight
And sings and romps,
Bringing him on
The shadowy hare
For him to rend
And deal a death
That he nor it
(Nor I) have wit
To comprehend.

IT IS ALMOST THE YEAR
TWO THOUSAND

To start the world of old
We had one age of gold
Not labored out of mines,
And some say there are signs
The second such has come,
The true Millennium,
The final golden glow
To end it. And if so
(And science ought to know)
We well may raise our heads
From weeding garden beds
And annotating books
To watch this end de luxe.

IN A POEM

The sentencing goes blithely on its way,
And takes the playfully objected rhyme
As surely as it keeps the stroke and time
In having its undeviable say.

ON OUR SYMPATHY WITH
THE UNDER DOG

First under up and then again down under,
We watch a circus of revolving dogs
No senator dares in to kick asunder
Lest both should bite him in the toga-togs.

A QUESTION

A voice said, Look me in the stars
And tell me truly, men of earth,
If all the soul-and-body scars
Were not too much to pay for birth.

BOEOTIAN

I love to toy with the Platonic notion
That wisdom need not be of Athens Attic,
But well may be Laconic, even Boeotian.
At least I will not have it systematic.

THE SECRET SITS

We dance round in a ring and suppose,
But the Secret sits in the middle and knows.

A SEMI-REVOLUTION

I advocate a semi-revolution.
The trouble with a total revolution
(Ask any reputable Rosicrucian)
Is that it brings the same class up on top.
Executives of skillful execution
Will therefore plan to go halfway and stop.
Yes, revolutions are the only salves,
But they're one thing that should be done by halves.

AN ANSWER

But Islands of the Blessèd, bless you, son,
I never came upon a blessèd one.

TRESPASS

No, I had set no prohibiting sign,
And yes, my land was hardly fenced.
Nevertheless the land was mine:
I was being trespassed on and against.

Whoever the surly freedom took
Of such an unaccountable stay
Busying by my woods and brook
Gave me strangely restless day.

He might be opening leaves of stone,
The picture-book of the trilobite,
For which the region round was known,
And in which there was little property right.

'Twas not the value I stood to lose
In specimen crab in specimen rock,
But his ignoring what was whose
That made me look again at the clock.

Then came his little acknowledgment:
He asked for a drink at the kitchen door,
An errand he may have had to invent,
But it made my property mine once more.

OF THE STONES OF THE PLACE

I farm a pasture where the boulders lie
As touching as a basket full of eggs,

And though they're nothing anybody begs,
I wonder if it wouldn't signify

For me to send you one out where you live
In wind-soil to a depth of thirty feet,
And every acre good enough to eat,
As fine as flour put through a baker's sieve.

I'd ship a smooth one you could slap and chafe,
And set up like a statue in your yard,
An eolith palladium to guard
The West and keep the old tradition safe.

Carve nothing on it. You can simply say
In self-defense to quizzical inquiry:
'The portrait of the soul of my gransir Ira.
It came from where he came from anyway.'

A SERIOUS STEP LIGHTLY TAKEN

Between two burrs on the map
Was a hollow-headed snake.
The burrs were hills, the snake was a stream,
And the hollow head was a lake.

And the dot in *front* of a name
Was what should be a town.
And there might be a house we could buy
For only a dollar down.

With two wheels low in the ditch
We left our boiling car,
And knocked at the door of a house we found,
And there today we are.

A Witness Tree

It is turning three hundred years
In our cisatlantic shore
For family after family name.
We'll make it three hundred more

For our name farming here,
Aloof yet not aloof,
Enriching soil and increasing stock,
Repairing fence and roof;

A hundred thousand days
Of front-page paper events,
A half a dozen major wars,
And forty-five presidents.

Steeple Bush

A YOUNG BIRCH

The birch begins to crack its outer sheath
Of baby green and show the white beneath,
As whosoever likes the young and slight
May well have noticed. Soon entirely white
To double day and cut in half the dark
It will stand forth, entirely white in bark,
And nothing but the top a leafy green—
The only native tree that dares to lean,
Relying on its beauty, to the air.
(Less brave perhaps than trusting are the fair.)
And someone reminiscent will recall
How once in cutting brush along the wall
He spared it from the number of the slain,
At first to be no bigger than a cane,
And then no bigger than a fishing pole,
But now at last so obvious a bole
The most efficient help you ever hired
Would know that it was there to be admired,

And zeal would not be thanked that cut it down
When you were reading books or out of town.
It was a thing of beauty and was sent
To live its life out as an ornament.

SOMETHING FOR HOPE

At the present rate it must come to pass
And that right soon that the meadow sweet
And steeple bush not good to eat
Will have crowded out the edible grass.

Then all there is to do is wait
For maple birch and spruce to push
Through meadow sweet and steeple bush
And crowd them out at a similar rate.

No plow among these rocks would pay.
So busy yourself with other things
While the trees put on their wooden rings
And with long-sleeved branches hold their sway.

Then cut down the trees when lumber grown,
And there's your pristine earth all freed
From lovely blooming but wasteful weed
And ready again for the grass to own.

A cycle we'll say of a hundred years.
Thus foresight does it and laissez faire,
A virtue in which we all may share
Unless a government interferes.

Patience and looking away ahead,
And leaving some things to take their course.
Hope may not nourish a cow or horse,
But spes alit agricolam 'tis said.

ONE STEP BACKWARD TAKEN

Not only sands and gravels
Were once more on their travels,
But gulping muddy gallons
Great boulders off their balance
Bumped heads together dully
And started down the gully.
Whole capes caked off in slices.
I felt my standpoint shaken
In the universal crisis.
But with one step backward taken
I saved myself from going.
A world torn loose went by me.
Then the rain stopped and the blowing
And the sun came out to dry me.

DIRECTIVE

Back out of all this now too much for us,
Back in a time made simple by the loss
Of detail, burned, dissolved, and broken off
Like graveyard marble sculpture in the weather,
There is a house that is no more a house
Upon a farm that is no more a farm
And in a town that is no more a town.
The road there, if you'll let a guide direct you

Steeple Bush

Who only has at heart your getting lost,
May seem as if it should have been a quarry—
Great monolithic knees the former town
Long since gave up pretense of keeping covered.
And there's a story in a book about it:
Besides the wear of iron wagon wheels
The ledges show lines ruled southeast northwest,
The chisel work of an enormous Glacier
That braced his feet against the Arctic Pole.
You must not mind a certain coolness from him
Still said to haunt this side of Panther Mountain.
Nor need you mind the serial ordeal
Of being watched from forty cellar holes
As if by eye pairs out of forty firkins.
As for the woods' excitement over you
That sends light rustle rushes to their leaves,
Charge that to upstart inexperience.
Where were they all not twenty years ago?
They think too much of having shaded out
A few old pecker-fretted apple trees.
Make yourself up a cheering song of how
Someone's road home from work this once was,
Who may be just ahead of you on foot
Or creaking with a buggy load of grain.
The height of the adventure is the height
Of country where two village cultures faded
Into each other. Both of them are lost.
And if you're lost enough to find yourself
By now, pull in your ladder road behind you
And put a sign up CLOSED to all but me.
Then make yourself at home. The only field
Now left's no bigger than a harness gall.
First there's the children's house of make believe,
Some shattered dishes underneath a pine,

To an Ancient

The playthings in the playhouse of the children.
Weep for what little things could make them glad.
Then for the house that is no more a house,
But only a belilaced cellar hole,
Now slowly closing like a dent in dough.
This was no playhouse but a house in earnest.
Your destination and your destiny's
A brook that was the water of the house,
Cold as a spring as yet so near its source,
Too lofty and original to rage.
(We know the valley streams that when aroused
Will leave their tatters hung on barb and thorn.)
I have kept hidden in the instep arch
Of an old cedar at the waterside
A broken drinking goblet like the Grail
Under a spell so the wrong ones can't find it,
So can't get saved, as Saint Mark says they mustn't.
(I stole the goblet from the children's playhouse.)
Here are your waters and your watering place.
Drink and be whole again beyond confusion.

TO AN ANCIENT

Your claims to immortality were two.
The one you made, the other one you grew.
Sorry to have no name for you but You.

We never knew exactly where to look,
But found one in the delta of a brook,
One in a cavern where you used to cook.

Coming on such an ancient human trace
Seems as expressive of the human race
As meeting someone living face to face.

Steeple Bush

We date you by your depth in silt and dust
Your probable brute nature is discussed.
At which point we are totally nonplussed.

You made the eolith, you grew the bone,
The second more peculiarly your own,
And likely to have been enough alone.

You make me ask if I would go to time
Would I gain anything by using rhyme?
Or aren't the bones enough I live to lime?

FIVE NOCTURNES

I. THE NIGHT LIGHT

She always had to burn a light
Beside her attic bed at night.
It gave bad dreams and broken sleep,
But helped the Lord her soul to keep.
Good gloom on her was thrown away.
It is on me by night or day,
Who have, as I suppose, ahead
The darkest of it still to dread.

II. WERE I IN TROUBLE

Where I could think of no thoroughfare,
Away on the mountain up far too high,
A blinding headlight shifted glare
And began to bounce down a granite stair
Like a star fresh fallen out of the sky.
And I away in my opposite wood
Am touched by that unintimate light
And made feel less alone than I rightly should,
For traveler there could do me no good
Were I in trouble with night tonight.

III. BRAVADO

Have I not walked without an upward look
Of caution under stars that very well
Might not have missed me when they shot and fell?
It was a risk I had to take—and took.

IV. ON MAKING CERTAIN ANYTHING
HAS HAPPENED

I could be worse employed
Than as watcher of the void
Whose part should be to tell
What star if any fell.

Suppose some seed-pearl sun
Should be the only one;
Yet still I must report
Some cluster one star short.

I should justly hesitate
To frighten church or state
By announcing a star down
From say the Cross or Crown.

To make sure what star I missed
I should have to check on my list
Every star in sight.
It might take me all night.

V. IN THE LONG NIGHT

I would build my house of crystal
With a solitary friend
Where the cold cracks like a pistol
And the needle stands on end.

We would pour oil on the ingle
And for want of books recite.
We would crawl out filing single
To observe the Northern Light.

V. In the Long Night

If Etookashoo and Couldlooktoo
The Esquimaux should call,
There would be fish raw and cooked too
And enough drink oil for all.

As one rankly warm insider
To another I would say,
We can rest assured on eider
There will come another day.

A SPIRE AND BELFRY

A MOOD APART

Once down on my knees to growing plants
I prodded the earth with a lazy tool
In time with a medley of sotto chants;
But becoming aware of some boys from school
Who had stopped outside the fence to spy,
I stopped my song and almost heart,
For any eye is an evil eye
That looks in on to a mood apart.

THE FEAR OF GOD

If you should rise from Nowhere up to Somewhere,
From being No one up to being Someone,
Be sure to keep repeating to yourself
You owe it to an arbitrary god
Whose mercy to you rather than to others
Won't bear too critical examination.
Stay unassuming. If for lack of license
To wear the uniform of who you are,
You should be tempted to make up for it
In a subordinating look or tone
Beware of coming too much to the surface,

And using for apparel what was meant
To be the curtain of the inmost soul.

THE FEAR OF MAN

As a girl no one gallantly attends
Sets forth for home at midnight from a friend's—
She tries to make it in one catch of breath,
And this is not because she thinks of death.
The city seems intoppling from a height,
But she can trust it not to fall tonight.
(It will be taken down before it falls.)
There scarcely is a light in all its walls
Except beside a safe inside a bank
(For which assurance Mammon is to thank).
But there are little street lights she should trust
So jewel steady in the wind and dust.
Her fear is being spoken by the rude
And having her exposure misconstrued.
May I in my brief bolt across the scene
Not be misunderstood in what I mean.

A STEEPLE ON THE HOUSE

What if it should turn out eternity
Was but the steeple on our house of life
That made our house of life a house of worship?
We do not go up there to sleep at night.
We do not go up there to live by day.
Nor need we ever go up there to live.
A spire and belfry coming on the roof
Means that a soul is coming on the flesh.

THE COURAGE TO BE NEW

I hear the world reciting
The mistakes of ancient men,
The brutality and fighting
They will never have again.

Heartbroken and disabled
In body and in mind
They renew talk of the fabled
Federation of Mankind.

But they're blessed with the acumen
To suspect the human trait
Was not the *basest* human
That made them militate.

They will tell you more as soon as
You tell them what to do
With their ever breaking newness
And their courage to be new.

IOTA SUBSCRIPT

Seek not in me the big I capital,
Nor yet the little dotted in me seek.
If I have in me any I at all,
'Tis the iota subscript of the Greek.

So small am I as an attention beggar.
The letter you will find me subscript to
Is neither alpha, eta, nor omega,
But upsilon which is the Greek for you.

THE MIDDLENESS OF THE ROAD

The road at the top of the rise
Seems to come to an end
And take off into the skies.
So at the distant bend

It seems to go into a wood,
The place of standing still
As long the trees have stood.
But say what Fancy will,

The mineral drops that explode
To drive my ton of car
Are limited to the road.
They deal with near and far,

But have almost nothing to do
With the absolute flight and rest
The universal blue
And local green suggest.

SKEPTIC

Far star that tickles for me my sensitive plate
And fries a couple of ebon atoms white,
I don't believe I believe a thing you state.
I put no faith in the seeming facts of light.

I don't believe I believe you're the last in space,
I don't believe you're anywhere near the last,
I don't believe what makes you red in the face
Is after explosion going away so fast.

The universe may or may not be very immense.
As a matter of fact there are times when I am apt
To feel it close in tight against my sense
Like a caul in which I was born and still am wrapped.

A ROGERS GROUP

How young and unassuming
They waited in the street,
With babies in their arms
And baggage at their feet.

A trolley car they hailed
Went by with clanging gong
Before they guessed the corner
They waited on was wrong.

And no one told them so
By way of traveler's aid,
No one was so far touched
By the Rogers Group they made.

ON BEING IDOLIZED

The wave sucks back and with the last of water
It wraps a wisp of seaweed round my legs,
And with the swift rush of its sandy dregs

So undermines my barefoot stand I totter
And did I not take steps would be tipped over
Like the ideal of some mistaken lover.

IT BIDS PRETTY FAIR

The play seems out for an almost infinite run.
Don't mind a little thing like the actors fighting.
The only thing I worry about is the sun.
We'll be all right if nothing goes wrong with the lighting.

A CLIFF DWELLING

There sandy seems the golden sky
And golden seems the sandy plain.
No habitation meets the eye
Unless in the horizon rim,
Some halfway up the limestone wall,
That spot of black is not a stain
Or shadow, but a cavern hole,
Where someone used to climb and crawl
To rest from his besetting fears.
I see the callus on his sole
The disappearing last of him
And of his race starvation slim,
Oh, years ago—ten thousand years.

A CASE FOR JEFFERSON

Harrison loves my country too,
But wants it all made over new.
He's Freudian Viennese by night.
By day he's Marxian Muscovite.

It isn't because he's Russian Jew.
He's Puritan Yankee through and through.
He dotes on Saturday pork and beans.
But his mind is hardly out of his teens:
With him the love of country means
Blowing it all to smithereens
And having it all made over new.

ETHEREALIZING

A theory if you hold it hard enough
And long enough gets rated as a creed:
Such as that flesh is something we can slough
So that the mind can be entirely freed.
Then when the arms and legs have atrophied,
And brain is all that's left of mortal stuff,
We can lie on the beach with the seaweed
And take our daily tide baths smooth and rough.
There once we lay as blobs of jellyfish
At evolution's opposite extreme.
But now as blobs of brain we'll lie and dream,
With only one vestigial creature wish:
Oh, may the tide be soon enough at high
To keep our abstract verse from being dry.

WHY WAIT FOR SCIENCE

Sarcastic Science she would like to know,
In her complacent ministry of fear,
How we propose to get away from here
When she has made things so we have to go
Or be wiped out. Will she be asked to show
Us how by rocket we may hope to steer
To some star off there say a half light-year
Through temperature of absolute zero?
Why wait for Science to supply the how

When any amateur can tell it now?
The way to go away should be the same
As fifty million years ago we came—
If anyone remembers how that was.
I have a theory, but it hardly does.

THE PLANNERS

If anything should put an end to This,
I'm thinking the unborn would never miss
What they had never had of vital bliss.
No burst of nuclear phenomenon
That put an end to what was going on
Could make much difference to the dead and gone.
Only a few of those even in whose day
It happened would have very much to say.
And anyone might ask them who were *they*.
Who *would* they be? The guild of social planners
With the intention blazoned on their banners
Of getting one more chance to change our manners?
These anyway might think it was important
That human history should not be shortened.

NO HOLY WARS FOR THEM

States strong enough to do good are but few.
Their number would seem limited to three.
Good is a thing that they the great can do,
But puny little states can only be.
And being good for these means standing by
To watch a war in nominal alliance,
And when it's over watch the world's supply

Get parceled out among the winning giants.
God, have you taken cognizance of this?
And what on this is your divine position?
That nations like the Cuban and the Swiss
Can never hope to wage a Global Mission.
No Holy Wars for them. The most the small
Can ever give us is a nuisance brawl.

U. S. 1946 KING'S X

Having invented a new Holocaust,
And been the first with it to win a war,
How they make haste to cry with fingers crossed,
King's X—no fairs to use it any more!

THE INGENUITIES OF DEBT

These I assume were words so deeply meant
They cut themselves in stone for permanent
Like trouble in the brow above the eyes:
'Take Care to Sell Your Horse before He Dies
The Art of Life Is Passing Losses on.'
The city saying it was Ctesiphon,
Which may a little while by war and trade
Have kept from being caught with the decayed,
Infirm, worn-out, and broken on its hands,
But judging by what little of it stands,
Not even the ingenuities of debt
Could save it from its losses being met.
Sand has been thrusting in the square of door
Across the tessellation of the floor,
And only rests, a serpent on its chin,

267

Content with contemplating, taking in,
Till it can muster breath inside a hall
To rear against the inscription on the wall.

TO THE RIGHT PERSON

In the one state of ours that is a shire,
There is a District Schoolhouse I admire
As much as anything for situation.
There are few institutions standing higher
This side the Rockies in my estimation—
Two thousand feet above the ocean level.
It has two entries for coeducation.
But there's a tight shut look to either door
And to the windows of its fenestration,
As if to say mere learning was the devil
And this school wasn't keeping any more
Unless for penitents who took their seat
Upon its doorsteps as at mercy's feet
To make up for a lack of meditation.

An Afterword

TAKE SOMETHING LIKE A STAR

O Star (the fairest one in sight),
We grant your loftiness the right
To some obscurity of cloud—
It will not do to say of night,
Since dark is what brings out your light.
Some mystery becomes the proud.
But to be wholly taciturn
In your reserve is not allowed.
Say something to us we can learn
By heart and when alone repeat.
Say something! And it says, 'I burn.'
But say with what degree of heat.
Talk Fahrenheit, talk Centigrade.
Use language we can comprehend.
Tell us what elements you blend.
It gives us strangely little aid,
But does tell something in the end.
And steadfast as Keats' Eremite,

Not even stooping from its sphere,
It asks a little of us here.
It asks of us a certain height,
So when at times the mob is swayed
To carry praise or blame too far,
We may take something like a star
To stay our minds on and be staid.

CLOSED FOR GOOD

Much as I own I owe
The passers of the past
Because their to and fro
Has cut this road to last,
I owe them more today
Because they've gone away

And come not back with steed
And chariot to chide
My slowness with their speed
And scare me to one side.
They have found other scenes
For haste and other means.

They leave the road to me
To walk in saying naught
Perhaps but to a tree
Inaudibly in thought,
'From you the road receives
A priming coat of leaves.

'And soon for lack of sun,
The prospects are in white

Closed for Good

It will be further done,
But with a coat so light
The shape of leaves will show
Beneath the brush of snow.'

And so on into winter
Till even I have ceased
To come as a foot printer,
And only some slight beast
So mousy or so foxy
Shall print there as my proxy.

A Masque of Reason

A MASQUE OF REASON

A fair oasis in the purest desert.
A man sits leaning back against a palm.
His wife lies by him looking at the sky.

MAN. You're not asleep?

WIFE. No, I can hear you. Why?

MAN. I said the incense tree's on fire again.

WIFE. You mean the Burning Bush?

MAN. The Christmas Tree.

WIFE. I shouldn't be surprised.

MAN. The strangest light!

WIFE. There's a strange light on everything today.

MAN. The myrrh tree gives it. Smell the rosin burning?
The ornaments the Greek artificers

Made for the Emperor Alexius,
The Star of Bethlehem, the pomegranates,
The birds, seem all on fire with Paradise
And hark, the gold enameled nightingales
Are singing. Yes, and look, the Tree is troubled.
Someone's caught in the branches.

WIFE.   So there is.
He can't get out.

MAN.   He's loose! He's out!

WIFE.   It's God.
I'd know Him by Blake's picture anywhere.
Now what's He doing?

MAN.   Pitching throne, I guess,
Here by our atoll.

WIFE.   Something Byzantine.

(*The throne's a plywood flat, prefabricated,
That God pulls lightly upright on its hinges
And stands beside, supporting it in place.*)

Perhaps for an Olympic Tournament,
Or Court of Love.

MAN.   More likely Royal Court—
Or Court of Law, and this is Judgment Day.
I trust it is. Here's where I lay aside
My varying opinion of myself
And come to rest in an official verdict.
Suffer yourself to be admired, my love,
As Waller says.

WIFE.   Or not admired. Go over
And speak to Him before the others come.
Tell Him He may remember you: you're Job.

GOD. Oh, I remember well: you're Job, my Patient.
How are you now? I trust you're quite recovered,
And feel no ill effects from what I gave you.

JOB. Gave me in truth: I like the frank admission.
I am a name for being put upon.
But, yes, I'm fine, except for now and then
A reminiscent twinge of rheumatism.
The let-up's heavenly. You perhaps will tell us
If that is all there is to be of Heaven,
Escape from so great pains of life on earth
It gives a sense of let-up calculated
To last a fellow to Eternity.

GOD. Yes, by and by. But first a larger matter.
I've had you on my mind a thousand years
To thank you someday for the way you helped me
Establish once for all the principle
There's no connection man can reason out
Between his just deserts and what he gets.
Virtue may fail and wickedness succeed.
'Twas a great demonstration we put on.
I should have spoken sooner had I found
The word I wanted. You would have supposed
One who in the beginning *was* the Word
Would be in a position to command it.
I have to wait for words like anyone.
Too long I've owed you this apology
For the apparently unmeaning sorrow
You were afflicted with in those old days.
But it was of the essence of the trial
You shouldn't understand it at the time.
It had to seem unmeaning to have meaning.
And it came out all right. I have no doubt
You realize by now the part you played

To stultify the Deuteronomist
And change the tenor of religious thought.
My thanks are to you for releasing me
From moral bondage to the human race.
The only free will there at first was man's,
Who could do good or evil as he chose.
I had no choice but I must follow him
With forfeits and rewards he understood—
Unless I liked to suffer loss of worship.
I had to prosper good and punish evil.
You changed all that. You set me free to reign.
You are the Emancipator of your God,
And as such I promote you to a saint.

JOB. You hear him, Thyatira: we're a saint.
Salvation in our case is retroactive.
We're saved, we're saved, whatever else it means.

JOB'S WIFE. Well, after all these years!

JOB.   This is my wife.

JOB'S WIFE. If You're the deity I assume You are—
(I'd know You by Blake's picture anywhere)—

GOD. The best, I'm told, I ever have had taken.

JOB'S WIFE. —I have a protest I would lodge with You.
I want to ask You if it stands to reason
That women prophets should be burned as witches
Whereas men prophets are received with honor.

JOB. Except in their own country, Thyatira.

GOD. You're not a witch?

JOB'S WIFE.   No.

GOD.   Have you ever been one?

JOB. Sometimes she thinks she has and gets herself
Worked up about it. But she really hasn't—
Not in the sense of having to my knowledge
Predicted anything that came to pass.

JOB'S WIFE. The witch of Endor was a friend of mine.

GOD. You wouldn't say she fared so very badly.
I noticed when she called up Samuel
His spirit had to come. Apparently
A witch was stronger than a prophet there.

JOB'S WIFE. But she was burned for witchcraft.

GOD.   That is not
Of record in my Note Book.

JOB'S WIFE.   Well, she was.
And I should like to know the reason why.

GOD. There you go asking for the very thing
We've just agreed I didn't have to give.

   (*The throne collapses. But He picks it up
   And this time locks it up and leaves it.*)

Where has she been the last half hour or so?
She wants to know why there is still injustice.
I answer flatly: That's the way it is,
And bid my will avouch it like Macbeth.
We may as well go back to the beginning
And look for justice in the case of Segub.

JOB. Oh, Lord, let's not go *back* to anything.

GOD. Because your wife's past won't bear looking into?
In our great moment what did you do, Madam?
What did you try to make your husband say?

JOB'S WIFE. No, let's not live things over. I don't care.

I stood by Job. I may have turned on You.
Job scratched his boils and tried to think what he
Had done or not done to or for the poor.
The test is always how we treat the poor.
It's time the poor were treated by the state
In some way not so penal as the poorhouse.
That's one thing more to put on Your agenda.
Job hadn't done a thing, poor innocent.
I told him not to scratch: it made it worse.
If I said once I said a thousand times,
Don't scratch! And when, as rotten as his skin,
His tents blew all to pieces, I picked up
Enough to build him every night a pup tent
Around him so it wouldn't touch and hurt him.
I did my wifely duty. I should tremble!
All You can seem to do is lose Your temper
When reason-hungry mortals ask for reasons.
Of course, in the abstract high singular
There isn't any universal reason;
And no one but a man would think there was.
You don't catch women trying to be Plato.
Still there must be lots of unsystematic
Stray scraps of palliative reason
It wouldn't hurt You to vouchsafe the faithful.
You thought it was agreed You needn't give them.
You thought to suit Yourself. I've not agreed
To anything with anyone.

JOB.   There, there,
You go to sleep. God must await events
As well as words.

JOB'S WIFE.   I'm serious. God's had
Aeons of time and still it's mostly women
Get burned for prophecy, men almost never.

JOB. God needs time just as much as you or I
To get things done. Reformers fail to see that.
She'll go to sleep. Nothing keeps her awake
But physical activity, I find.
Try to read to her and she drops right off.

GOD. She's beautiful.

JOB.   Yes, she was just remarking
She now felt younger by a thousand years
Than the day she was born.

GOD.   That's about right,
I should have said. You got your age reversed
When time was found to be a space dimension
That could, like any space, be turned around in?

JOB. Yes, both of us: we saw to that at once.
But, God, I have a question too to raise.
(My wife gets in ahead of me with hers.)
I need some help about this reason problem
Before I am too late to be got right
As to what reasons I agree to waive.
I'm apt to string along with Thyatira.
God knows—or rather, You know (God forgive me)
I waived the reason for my ordeal—but—
I have a question even there to ask—
In confidence. There's no one here but her,
And she's a woman: she's not interested
In general ideas and principles.

GOD. What are her interests, Job?

JOB.   Witch-women's rights.
Humor her there or she will be confirmed
In her suspicion You're no feminist.
You have it in for women, she believes.

Kipling invokes You as Lord God of Hosts.
She'd like to know how You would take a prayer
That started off Lord God of Hostesses.

GOD. I'm charmed with her.

JOB.   Yes, I could see You were.
But to my question. I am much impressed
With what You say we have established.
Between us, You and I.

GOD.   I make you see?
It would be too bad if Columbus-like
You failed to see the worth of your achievement.

JOB. You call it mine.

GOD.   We groped it out together.
Any originality it showed
I give you credit for. My forte is truth,
Or metaphysics, long the world's reproach
For standing still in one place true forever;
While science goes self-superseding on.
Look at how far we've left the current science
Of Genesis behind. The wisdom there though,
Is just as good as when I uttered it.
Still, novelty has doubtless an attraction.

JOB. So it's important who first thinks of things?

GOD. I'm a great stickler for the author's name.
By proper names I find I do my thinking.

JOB'S WIFE. God, who invented earth?

JOB.   What, still awake?

GOD. Any originality it showed
Was of the Devil. He invented Hell,

279

False premises that are the original
Of all originality, the sin
That felled the angels, Wolsey should have said.
As for the earth, we groped that out together,
Much as your husband Job and I together
Found out the discipline man needed most
Was to learn his submission to unreason;
And that for man's own sake as well as mine,
So he won't find it hard to take his orders
From his inferiors in intelligence
In peace and war—especially in war.

JOB. So he won't find it hard to take his war.

GOD. You have the idea. There's not much I can tell **you.**

JOB. All very splendid. I am flattered proud
To have been in on anything with You.
'Twas a great demonstration if You say so.
Though incidentally I sometimes wonder
Why it had had to be at my expense.

GOD. It had to be at somebody's expense.
Society can never think things out:
It has to see them acted out by actors,
Devoted actors at a sacrifice—
The ablest actors I can lay **my** hands on.
Is that your answer?

JOB.   No, for I have yet
To ask my question. We disparage reason.
But all the time it's what we're most concerned with.
There's will as motor and there's will as brakes.
Reason is, I suppose, the steering gear.
The will as brakes can't stop the will as motor
For very long. We're plainly made to go.

We're going anyway and may as well
Have some say as to where we're headed for;
Just as we will be talking anyway
And may as well throw in a little sense.
Let's do so now. Because I let You off
From telling me Your reason, don't assume
I thought You had none. Somewhere back
I knew You had one. But this isn't it
You're giving me. You say we groped this out.
But if You will forgive me the irreverence,
It sounds to me as if You thought it out,
And took Your time to it. It seems to me
An afterthought, a long long afterthought.
I'd give more for one least beforehand reason
Than all the justifying ex-post-facto
Excuses trumped up by You for theologists.
The front of being answerable to no one
I'm with You in maintaining to the public.
But, Lord, we showed them what. The audience
Has all gone home to bed. The play's played out.
Come, after all these years—to satisfy me.
I'm curious. And I'm a grown-up man:
I'm not a child for You to put me off
And tantalize me with another 'Oh, because.'
You'd be the last to want me to believe
All Your effects were merely lucky blunders.
That would be unbelief and atheism.
The artist in me cries out for design,
Such devilish ingenuity of torture
Did seem unlike You, and I tried to think
The reason might have been some other person's.
But there is nothing You are not behind.
I did not ask then, but it seems as if
Now after all these years You might indulge me.

Why did You hurt me so? I am reduced
To asking flatly for the reason—outright.

GOD. I'd tell you, Job—

JOB.   All right, don't tell me then
If you don't want to. I don't want to know.
But what is all this secrecy about?
I fail to see what fun, what satisfaction
A God can find in laughing at how badly
Men fumble at the possibilities
When left to guess forever for themselves.
The chances are when there's so much pretense
Of metaphysical profundity
The obscurity's a fraud to cover nothing.
I've come to think no so-called hidden value's
Worth going after. Get down into things
It will be found there's no more given there
Than on the surface. If there ever was,
The crypt was long since rifled by the Greeks.
We don't know where we are, or who we are.
We don't know one another; don't know you;
Don't know what time it is. We don't know, don't we?
Who says we don't? Who got up these misgivings?
Oh, we know well enough to go ahead with.
I mean we seem to know enough to act on.
It comes down to a doubt about the wisdom
Of having children—after having had them,
So there is nothing we can do about it
But warn the children they perhaps should have none.
You could end this by simply coming out
And saying plainly and unequivocally
Whether there's any part of man immortal.
Yet You don't speak. Let fools bemuse themselves
By being baffled for the sake of being.

I'm sick of the whole artificial puzzle.

JOB'S WIFE. You won't get any answers out of God.

GOD. My kingdom, what an outbreak!

JOB'S WIFE.   Job is right.
Your kingdom, yes, Your kingdom come on earth.
Pray tell me what does that mean. Anything?
Perhaps that earth is going to crack someday
Like a big egg and hatch a heaven out
Of all the dead and buried from their graves.
One simple little statement from the throne
Would put an end to such fantastic nonsense;
And, too, take care of twenty of the four
And twenty freedoms on the party docket.
Or is it only four? My extra twenty
Are freedoms from the need of asking questions.
(I hope You know the game called twenty questions.)
For instance, is there such a thing as Progress?
Job says there's no such thing as Earth's becoming
An easier place for man to save his soul in.
Except as a hard place to save his soul in,
A trial ground where he can try himself
And find out whether he is any good,
It would be meaningless. It might as well
Be Heaven at once and have it over with.

GOD. Two pitching on like this tend to confuse me.
One at a time, please. I will answer Job first.
I'm going to tell Job why I tortured him
And trust it won't be adding to the torture.
I was just showing off to the Devil, Job,
As is set forth in chapters One and Two.
(*Job takes a few steps pacing.*) Do you mind?
(*God eyes him anxiously.*)

JOB.   No. No, I mustn't.
'Twas human of You. I expected more
Than I could understand and what I get
Is almost less than I can understand.
But I don't mind. Let's leave it as it stood.
The point was it was none of my concern.
I stick to that. But talk about confusion!
How is that for a mix-up, Thyatira?
Yet I suppose what seems to us confusion
Is not confusion, but the form of forms,
The serpent's tail stuck down the serpent's throat,
Which is the symbol of eternity
And also of the way all things come round,
Or of how rays return upon themselves,
To quote the greatest Western poem yet.
Though I hold rays deteriorate to nothing,
First white, then red, then ultra red, then out.

GOD. Job, you must understand my provocation.
The tempter comes to me and I am tempted.
I'd had about enough of his derision
Of what I valued most in human nature.
He thinks he's smart. He thinks he can convince me
It is no different with my followers
From what it is with his. Both serve for pay.
Disinterestedness never did exist
And if it did, it wouldn't be a virtue.
Neither would fairness. You have heard the doctrine.
It's on the increase. He could count on no one:
That was his look out. I could count on you.
I wanted him forced to acknowledge so much.
I gave you over to him, but with safeguards.
I took care of you. And before you died
I trust I made it clear I took your side

Against your comforters in their contention
You must be wicked to déserve such pain.
That's Browning and sheer Chapel Non-conformism.

JOB. God, please. enough for now. I'm in no mood
For more excuses.

GOD.   What I mean to say:
Your comforters were wrong.

JOB.   Oh, that committee!

GOD. I saw you had no fondness for committees.
Next time you find yourself pressed on to one
For the revision of the Book of Prayer
Put that in if it isn't in already:
Deliver us from committees. 'Twill remind me.
I would do anything for you in reason.

JOB. Yes, yes.

GOD.   You don't seem satisfied.

JOB.   I am.

GOD. You're pensive.

JOB.   Oh, I'm thinking of the Devil.
You must remember he was in on this.
We can't leave him out.

GOD.   No. No, we don't need to.
We're too well off.

JOB.   Someday we three should have
A good old get-together celebration.

GOD. Why not right now?

JOB.   We can't without the Devil.

GOD. The Devil's never very far away.
He too is pretty circumambient.
He has but to appear. He'll come for me,
Precipitated from the desert air.
Show yourself, son. I'll get back on my throne
For this I think. I find it always best
To be upon my dignity with him.

> (*The Devil enters like a sapphire wasp*
> *That flickers mica wings. He lifts a hand*
> *To brush away a disrespectful smile.*
> *Job's wife sits up.*)

JOB'S WIFE.   Well, if we aren't all here.
Including me, the only Dramatis
Personae needed to enact the problem.

JOB. We've waked her up.

JOB'S WIFE.   I haven't been asleep.
I've heard what you were saying—every word.

JOB. What did we say?

JOB'S WIFE.   You said the Devil's in it.

JOB. She always claims she hasn't been asleep.
And what else did we say?

JOB'S WIFE.   Well, what led up—
Something about— (*The three men laugh.*)
—The Devil's being God's best inspiration.

JOB. Good, pretty good.

JOB'S WIFE.   Wait till I get my Kodak.
Would you two please draw in a little closer?
No—no, that's not a smile there. That's a grin.
Satan, what ails you? Where's the famous tongue,

Thou onetime Prince of Conversationists?
This is polite society you're in
Where good and bad are mingled everywhichway,
And ears are lent to any sophistry
Just as if nothing mattered but our manners.
You look as if you either hoped or feared
You were more guilty of mischief than you are.
Nothing has been brought out that for my part
I'm not prepared for or that Job himself
Won't find a formula for taking care of.

SATAN. Like the one Milton found to fool himself
About his blindness.

JOB'S WIFE.   Oh, he speaks! He *can* speak!
That strain again! Give me excess of it!
As dulcet as a pagan temple gong!
He's twitting us. Oh, by the way, you haven't
By any chance a Lady Apple on you?
I saw a boxful in the Christmas market.
How I should prize one personally from you.

GOD. Don't *you* twit. He's unhappy. Church neglect
And figurative use have pretty well
Reduced him to a shadow of himself.

JOB'S WIFE. *That* explains why he's so diaphanous
And easy to see through. But where's he off to?
I thought there were to be festivities
Of some kind. We could have charades.

GOD. He has his business he must be about.
Job mentioned him and so I brought him in
More to give his reality its due
Than anything.

JOB'S WIFE.   He's very real to me

And always will be. Please don't go. Stay, stay
But to the evensong and having played
Together we will go with you along.
There are who won't have had enough of you
If you go now. Look how he takes no steps!
He isn't really going, yet he's leaving.

JOB. (*Who has been standing dazed with new ideas*)
He's on that tendency that like the Gulf Stream,
Only of sand not water, runs through here.
It has a rate distinctly different
From the surrounding desert; just today
I stumbled over it and got tripped up.

JOB'S WIFE. Oh, yes, that tendency! Oh, do come off it.
Don't let it carry you away. I hate
A tendency. The minute you get on one
It seems to start right off accelerating.
Here, take my hand.

        (*He takes it and alights*
  In three quick steps as off an escalator.
  The tendency, a long, long narrow strip
  Of middle-aisle church carpet, sisal hemp,
  Is worked by hands invisible off stage.)

I want you in my group beside the throne—
Must have you. There, that's just the right arrangement.
Now someone can light up the Burning Bush
And turn the gold enameled artificial birds on.
I recognize them. Greek artificers
Devised them for Alexius Comnenus.
They won't show in the picture. That's too bad.
Neither will I show. That's too bad moreover.
Now if you three have settled anything
You'd as well smile as frown on the occasion.

   (*Here endeth chapter forty-three of Job.*)

In the Clearing

POD OF THE MILKWEED

Calling all butterflies of every race
From source unknown but from no special place
They ever will return to all their lives,
Because unlike the bees they have no hives,
The milkweed brings up to my very door
The theme of wanton waste in peace and war
As it has never been to me before.
And so it seems a flower's coming out
That should if not be talked then sung about.
The countless wings that from the infinite
Make such a noiseless tumult over it
Do no doubt with their color compensate
For what the drab weed lacks of the ornate.
For drab it is its fondest must admit.
And yes, although it is a flower that flows
With milk and honey, it is bitter milk,

289

In the Clearing

As anyone who ever broke its stem
And dared to taste the wound a little knows.
It tastes as if it might be opiate.
But whatsoever else it may secrete,
Its flowers' distilled honey is so sweet
It makes the butterflies intemperate.
There is no slumber in its juice for them.
One knocks another off from where he clings.
They knock the dyestuff off each other's wings—
With thirst on hunger to the point of lust.
They raise in their intemperance a cloud
Of mingled butterfly and flower dust
That hangs perceptibly above the scene.
In being sweet to these ephemerals
The sober weed has managed to contrive
In our three hundred days and sixty five
One day too sweet for beings to survive.
Many shall come away as struggle worn
And spent and dusted off of their regalia
To which at daybreak they were freshly born
As after one-of-them's proverbial failure
From having beaten all day long in vain
Against the wrong side of a window pane.

But waste was of the essence of the scheme.
And all the good they did for man or god
To all those flowers they passionately trod
Was leave as their posterity one pod
With an inheritance of restless dream.
He hangs on upside down with talon feet
In an inquisitive position odd
As any Guatemalan parakeet.
Something eludes him. Is it food to eat?
Or some dim secret of the good of waste?

Away!

He almost has it in his talon clutch.
Where have those flowers and butterflies all gone
That science may have staked the future on?
He seems to say the reason why so much
Should come to nothing must be fairly faced.*

AWAY!

Now I out walking
The world desert,
And my shoe and my stocking
Do me no hurt.

I leave behind
Good friends in town.
Let them get well-wined
And go lie down.

Don't think I leave
For the outer dark
Like Adam and Eve
Put out of the Park.

Forget the myth.
There is no one I
Am put out with
Or put out by.

Unless I'm wrong
I but obey
The urge of a song:
I'm—bound—away!

---

* And shall be in due course.

And I may return
If dissatisfied
With what I learn
From having died.

A CABIN IN THE CLEARING

for Alfred Edwards

MIST. I don't believe the sleepers in this house
Know where they are.

SMOKE.   They've been here long enough
To push the woods back from around the house
And part them in the middle with a path.

MIST. And still I doubt if they know where they are.
And I begin to fear they never will.
All they maintain the path for is the comfort
Of visiting with the equally bewildered.
Nearer in plight their neighbors are than distance.

SMOKE. I am the guardian wraith of starlit smoke
That leans out this and that way from their chimney.
I will not have their happiness despaired of.

MIST. No one—not I—would give them up for lost
Simply because they don't know where they are.
I am the damper counterpart of smoke
That gives off from a garden ground at night
But lifts no higher than a garden grows.
I cotton to their landscape. That's who I am.
I am no further from their fate than you are.

SMOKE. They must by now have learned the native tongue.
Why don't they ask the Red Man where they are?

MIST. They often do, and none the wiser for it.
So do they also ask philosophers
Who come to look in on them from the pulpit.
They will ask anyone there is to ask—
In the fond faith accumulated fact
Will of itself take fire and light the world up.
Learning has been a part of their religion.

SMOKE. If the day ever comes when they know who
They are, they may know better where they are.
But who they are is too much to believe—
Either for them or the onlooking world.
They are too sudden to be credible.

MIST. Listen, they murmur talking in the dark
On what should be their daylong theme continued.
Putting the lamp out has not put their thought out.
Let us pretend the dewdrops from the eaves
Are you and I eavesdropping on their unrest—
A mist and smoke eavesdropping on a haze—
And see if we can tell the bass from the soprano.

Than smoke and mist who better could appraise
The kindred spirit of an inner haze.

AMERICA IS HARD TO SEE

Columbus may have worked the wind
A new and better way to Ind
And also proved the world a ball,
But how about the wherewithal?
Not just for scientific news
Had the Queen backed him to a cruise.

In the Clearing

Remember he had made the test
Finding the East by sailing West.
But had he found it? Here he was
Without one trinket from Ormuz
To save the Queen from family censure
For her investment in his venture.

There had been something strangely wrong
With every coast he tried along.
He could imagine nothing barrener.
The trouble was with him the mariner.
He wasn't off a mere degree;
His reckoning was off a sea.

And to intensify the drama
Another mariner, Da Gama,
Came just then sailing into port
From the same general resort,
And with the gold in hand to show for
His claim it was another Ophir.

Had but Columbus known enough
He might have boldly made the bluff
That better than Da Gama's gold
He had been given to behold
The race's future trial place,
A fresh start for the human race.

He might have fooled Valladolid.
I was deceived by what he did.
If I had had my chance when young
I should have had Columbus sung
As a god who had given us
A more than Moses' exodus.

But all he did was spread the room
Of our enacting out the doom
Of being in each other's way,
And so put off the weary day
When we would have to put our mind
On how to crowd but still be kind.

For these none too apparent gains
He got no more than dungeon chains
And such small posthumous renown
(A country named for him, a town,
A holiday) as where he is
He may not recognize for his.

They say his flagship's unlaid ghost
Still probes and dents our rocky coast
With animus approaching hate,
And for not turning out a strait,
He has cursed every river mouth
From fifty North to fifty South.

Some day our navy, I predict,
Will take in tow this derelict
And lock him through Culebra Cut,
His eyes as good (or bad) as shut
To all the modern works of man
And all we call American.

America is hard to see.
Less partial witnesses than he
In book on book have testified
They could not see it from outside—
Or inside either for that matter.
We know the literary chatter.

Columbus, as I say, will miss
All he owes to the artifice
Of tractor-plow and motor-drill.
To naught but his own force of will,
Or at most some Andean quake,
Will he ascribe this lucky break.

High purpose makes the hero rude;
He will not stop for gratitude.
But let him show his haughty stern
To what was never his concern
Except as it denied him way
To fortune-hunting in Cathay

He will be starting pretty late.
He'll find that Asiatic state
Is about tired of being looted
While having its beliefs disputed.
His can be no such easy raid
As Cortez on the Aztecs made.

PERIL OF HOPE

It is right in there
Betwixt and between
The orchard bare
And the orchard green,

When the boughs are right
In a flowery burst
Of pink and white,
That we fear the worst.

> For there's not a clime
> But at any cost
> Will take that time
> For a night of frost.

For John F. Kennedy His Inauguration

GIFT OUTRIGHT OF
"THE GIFT OUTRIGHT"

With Some Preliminary History in Rhyme

Summoning artists to participate
In the august occasions of the state
Seems something artists ought to celebrate.
Today is for my cause a day of days.
And his be poetry's old-fashioned praise
Who was the first to think of such a thing.
This verse that in acknowledgment I bring
Goes back to the beginning of the end
Of what had been for centuries the trend;
A turning point in modern history.
Colonial had been the thing to be
As long as the great issue was to see
What country'd be the one to dominate
By character, by tongue, by native trait,
The new world Christopher Columbus found.
The French, the Spanish, and the Dutch were downed
And counted out. Heroic deeds were done.
Elizabeth the First and England won.
Now came on a new order of the ages
That in the Latin of our founding sages
(Is it not written on the dollar bill

We carry in our purse and pocket still?)
God nodded his approval of as good.
So much those heroes knew and understood,
I mean the great four, Washington,
John Adams, Jefferson, and Madison,—
So much they knew as consecrated seers
They must have seen ahead what now appears,
They would bring empires down about our ears
And by the example of our Declaration
Make everybody want to be a nation.
And this is no aristocratic joke
At the expense of negligible folk.
We see how seriously the races swarm
In their attempts at sovereignty and form.
They are our wards we think to some extent
For the time being and with their consent,
To teach them how Democracy is meant.
"New order of the ages" did we say?
If it looks none too orderly today,
'Tis a confusion it was ours to start
So in it have to take courageous part.
No one of honest feeling would approve
A ruler who pretended not to love
A turbulence he had the better of.
Everyone knows the glory of the twain
Who gave America the aeroplane
To ride the whirlwind and the hurricane.
Some poor fool has been saying in his heart
Glory is out of date in life and art.
Our venture in revolution and outlawry
Has justified itself in freedom's story
Right down to now in glory upon glory.
Come fresh from an election like the last,
The greatest vote a people ever cast,

So close yet sure to be abided by,
It is no miracle our mood is high.
Courage is in the air in bracing whiffs
Better than all the stalemate an's and ifs.
There was the book of profile tales declaring
For the emboldened politicians daring
To break with followers when in the wrong,
A healthy independence of the throng,
A democratic form of right divine
To rule first answerable to high design.
There is a call to life a little sterner,
And braver for the earner, learner, yearner.
Less criticism of the field and court
And more preoccupation with the sport.
It makes the prophet in us all presage
The glory of a next Augustan age
Of a power leading from its strength and pride,
Of young ambition eager to be tried,
Firm in our free beliefs without dismay,
In any game the nations want to play.
A golden age of poetry and power
Of which this noonday's the beginning hour.

THE GIFT OUTRIGHT*

The land was ours before we were the land's.
She was our land more than a hundred years
Before we were her people. She was ours
In Massachusetts, in Virginia,
But we were England's, still colonials,
Possessing what we still were unpossessed by,

* Originally published in *Two or More*.

In the Clearing

Possessed by what we now no more possessed.
Something we were withholding made us weak
Until we found out that it was ourselves
We were withholding from our land of living,
And forthwith found salvation in surrender.
Such as we were we gave ourselves outright
(The deed of gift was many deeds of war)
To the land vaguely realizing westward,
But still unstoried, artless, unenhanced,
Such as she was, such as she would become.

A NEVER NAUGHT SONG

There was never naught,
There was always thought.
But when noticed first
It was fairly burst
Into having weight.
It was in a state
Of atomic One.
Matter was begun—
And in fact complete,
One and yet discrete
To conflict and pair.
Everything was there
Every single thing
Waiting was to bring,
Clear from hydrogen
All the way to men.
It is all the tree
It will ever be,
Bole and branch and root
Cunningly minute.
And this gist of all
Is so infra-small
As to blind our eyes
To its every guise
And so render nil
The whole Yggdrasil.
Out of coming-in
Into having been!
So the picture's caught

In the Clearing

Almost next to naught
But the force of thought.

A CONCEPT SELF-CONCEIVED

The latest creed that has to be believed
And entered in our childish catechism
Is that the All's a concept self-conceived,
Which is no more than good old Pantheism.

Great is the reassurance of recall.
Why go on further with confusing voice
To say God's either All or over all?
The rule is, never give a child a choice.

Forgive, O Lord, my little jokes on Thee
And I'll forgive Thy great big one on me.

KITTY HAWK

Back there in 1953 with the Huntington Cairnses
(A Skylark for Them in Three-Beat Phrases)

PART ONE

Portents, Presentiments,
and Premonitions

Kitty Hawk, O Kitty,
There was once a song,
Who knows but a great

Kitty Hawk

Emblematic ditty,
I might well have sung
When I came here young
Out and down along
Past Elizabeth City
Sixty years ago.
I was, to be sure,
Out of sorts with Fate,
Wandering to and fro
In the earth alone,
You might think too poor-
Spirited to care
Who I was or where
I was being blown
Faster than my tread—
Like the crumpled, better
Left-unwritten letter
I had read and thrown.
Oh, but not to boast,
Ever since Nag's Head
Had my heart been great,
Not to claim elate,
With a need the gale
Filled me with to shout
Summary riposte
To the dreary wail
There's no knowing what
Love is all about.
Poets know a lot.
Never did I fail
Of an answer back
To the zodiac
When in heartless chorus
Aries and Taurus,

In the Clearing

Gemini and Cancer
Mocked me for an answer.
It was on my tongue
To have up and sung
The initial flight
I can see now might—
Should have been my own—
Into the unknown,
Into the sublime
Off these sands of Time
Time had seen amass
From his hourglass.
Once I told the Master,
Later when we met,
I'd been here one night
As a young Alastor
When the scene was set
For some kind of flight
Long before he flew it.
Just supposing I—
I had beat him to it.
What did men mean by
THE original?
Why was it so very,
Very necessary
To be first of all?
How about the lie
That he wasn't first?
I was glad he laughed.
There was such a lie
Money and maneuver
Fostered over long
Until Herbert Hoover
Raised this tower shaft

Kitty Hawk

To undo the wrong.
Of all crimes the worst
Is to steal the glory
From the great and brave,
Even more accursed
Than to rob the grave.
But the sorry story
Has been long redressed.
And as for my jest
I had any claim
To the runway's fame
Had I only sung,
That is all my tongue.
I can't make it seem
More than that my theme
Might have been a dream
Of dark Hatteras
Or sad Roanoke,
One more fond alas
For the seed of folk
Sowed in vain by Raleigh,
Raleigh of the cloak,
And some other folly.

Getting too befriended,
As so often, ended
Any melancholy
Götterdämmerung
That I might have sung.
I fell in among
Some kind of committee
From Elizabeth City,
Each and every one
Loaded with a gun

Or a demijohn.
(Need a body ask
If it was a flask?)
Out to kill a duck
Or perhaps a swan
Over Currituck.
This was not their day
Anything to slay
Unless one another.
But their lack of luck
Made them no less gay
No, nor less polite.
They included me
Like a little brother
In their revelry—
All concern to take
Care my innocence
Should at all events
Tenderly be kept
For good gracious' sake.
And if they were gentle
They were sentimental.
One drank to his mother
While another wept.
Something made it sad
For me to break loose
From the need they had
To make themselves glad
They were of no use.
Manners made it hard,
But that night I stole
Off on the unbounded
Beaches where the whole
Of the Atlantic pounded.

Kitty Hawk

There I next fell in
With a lone coast guard
On midnight patrol,
Who as of a sect
Asked about my soul
And where-all I'd been.
Apropos of sin,
Did I recollect
How the wreckers wrecked
Theodosia Burr
Off this very shore?
'Twas to punish her,
But her father more—
We don't know what for:
There was no confession.
Things they think she wore
Still sometimes occur
In someone's possession
Here at Kitty Hawk.
We can have no notion
Of the strange devotion
Burr had for his daughter:
He was too devoted.
So it was in talk
We prolonged the walk,
On one side the ocean,
And on one a water
Of the inner sound;
"And the moon was full,"
As the poet said
And I aptly quoted.
And its being full
And right overhead,
Small but strong and round,

By its tidal pull
Made all being full.
Kitty Hawk, O Kitty,
Here it was again
In the selfsame day,
I at odds with men
Came upon their pity,
Equally profound
For a son astray
And a daughter drowned.

PART TWO

When the chance went by
For my Muse to fly
From this Runway Beach
As a figure of speech
In a flight of words,
Little I imagined
Men would treat this sky
Some day to a pageant
Like a thousand birds.
Neither you nor I
Ever thought to fly.
Oh, but fly we did,
Literally fly.
That's because though mere
Lilliputians we're
What Catullus called
Somewhat (aliquid).
Mind you, we are mind.
We are not the kind
To stay too confined.
After having crawled
Round the place on foot

Kitty Hawk

And done yeoman share
Of just staying put,
We arose from there
And we scaled a plane
So the stilly air
Almost pulled our hair
Like a hurricane.

Then I saw it all.

Pulpiteers will censure
Our instinctive venture
Into what they call
The material
When we took that fall
From the apple tree.
But God's own descent
Into flesh was meant
As a demonstration
That the supreme merit
Lay in risking spirit
In substantiation.
Westerners inherit
A design for living
Deeper into matter—
Not without due patter
Of a great misgiving.
All the science zest
To materialize
By on-penetration
Into earth and skies
(Don't forget the latter
Is but further matter)
Has been West Northwest.
If it was not wise,

In the Clearing

Tell me why the East
Seemingly has ceased
From its long stagnation
In mere meditation.
What is all the fuss
To catch up with us?
Can it be to flatter
Us with emulation?

Spirit enters flesh
And for all it's worth
Charges into earth
In birth after birth
Ever fresh and fresh.
We may take the view
That its derring-do
Thought of in the large
Was one mighty charge
On our human part
Of the soul's ethereal
Into the material.
In a running start
As it were from scratch
On a certain slab
Of (we'll say) basalt
In or near Moab
With intent to vault
In a vaulting match,
Never mind with whom—
(No one, I presume,
But ourselves—mankind,
In a love and hate
Rivalry combined.)
'Twas a radio

Voice that said, "Get set
In the alphabet,
That is A B C,
Which some day should be
Rhymed with 1 2 3
On a college gate."
Then the radio
Region voice said, "Go,
Go you on to know
More than you can sing.
Have no hallowing fears
Anything's forbidden
Just because it's hidden.
Trespass and encroach
On successive spheres
Without self-reproach."
Then for years and years
And for miles and miles
'Cross the Aegean Isles,
Athens Rome France Britain,
Always West Northwest,
As have I not written,
Till the so-long kept
Purpose was expressed
In the leap we leapt.
And the radio
Cried, "The Leap—The Leap!"
It belonged to US,
Not our friends the Russ,
To have run the event
To its full extent
And have won the crown,
Or let's say the cup,
On which with a date

In the Clearing

Is the inscription though,
"Nothing can go up
But it must come down."
Earth is still our fate.
The uplifted sight
We enjoyed at night
When instead of sheep
We were counting stars,
Not to go to sleep,
But to stay awake
For good gracious' sake,
Naming stars to boot
To avoid mistake,
Jupiter and Mars,
Just like Pullman cars,
'Twas no vain pursuit.
Some have preached and taught
All there was to thought
Was to master Nature
By some nomenclature.
But if not a law
'Twas an end foregone
Anything we saw
And thus fastened on
With an epithet
We would see to yet—
We would want to touch
Not to mention clutch.

Talk Aloft

Someone says the Lord
Says our reaching toward
Is its own reward.

Kitty Hawk

One would like to know
Where God says it though.

We don't like that much.

Let's see where we are.
What's that sulphur blur
Off there in the fog?
Go consult the log.
It's some kind of town,
But it's not New York.
We're not very far
Out from where we were.
It's still Kitty Hawk.

We'd have got as far
Even at a walk.

Don't you crash me down.
Though our kiting ships
Prove but flying chips
From the science shop
And when motors stop
They may have to drop
Short of anywhere,
Though our leap in air
Prove as vain a hop
As the hop from grass
Of a grasshopper,
Don't discount our powers;
We have made a pass
At the infinite,
Made it, as it were,
Rationally ours,

In the Clearing

To the most remote
Swirl of neon-lit
Particle afloat.
Ours was to reclaim
What had long been faced
As a fact of waste
And was waste in name.

That's how we became
Though an earth so small,
Justly known to fame
As the Capital
Of the universe.
We make no pretension
Of projecting ray
We can call our own
From this ball of stone,
None I don't reject
As too new to mention.
All we do's reflect
From our rocks, and yes,
From our brains no less.
And the better part
Is the ray we dart
From this head and heart,
The *mens animi*.

Till we came to be
There was not a trace
Of a thinking race
Anywhere in space.
We know of no world
Being whirled and whirled
Round and round the rink

Kitty Hawk

Of a single sun
(So as not to sink),
Not a single one
That has thought to think.

The Holiness
Of Wholeness

Pilot, though at best your
Flight is but a gesture,
And your rise and swoop,
But a loop the loop,
Lands on someone hard
In his own backyard
From no higher heaven
Than a bolt of levin,
I don't say retard.
Keep on elevating.
But while meditating
What we can's or can
Let's keep starring man
In the royal role.
It will not be his
Ever to create
One least germ or coal.
Those two things we can't.
But the comfort is
In the covenant
We may get control
If not of the whole
Of at least some part
Where not too immense,
So by craft or art
We can give the part

315

In the Clearing

Wholeness in a sense.
The becoming fear
That becomes us best
Is lest habit ridden
In the kitchen midden
Of our dump of earning
And our dump of learning
We come nowhere near
Getting thought expressed

The Mixture
Mechanic

This wide flight we wave
At the stars or moon
Means that we approve
Of them on the move.
Ours is to behave
Like a kitchen spoon
Of a size Titanic
To keep all things stirred
In a blend mechanic
Saying That's the tune,
That's the pretty kettle!
Matter mustn't curd,
Separate and settle.
Action is the word.

Nature's never quite
Sure she hasn't erred
In her vague design
Till on some fine night
We two come in flight
Like a king and queen

And by right divine,
Waving scepter-baton,
Undertake to tell her
What in being stellar
She's supposed to mean.

God of the machine,
Peregrine machine,
Some still think is Satan,
Unto you the thanks
For this token flight,
Thanks to you and thanks
To the brothers Wright
Once considered cranks
Like Darius Green
In their home town, Dayton.

ENDS

Loud talk in the overlighted house
That made us stumble past.
Oh, there had once been night the first,
But this was night the last.

Of all the things he might have said,
Sincere or insincere,
He never said she wasn't young,
And hadn't been his dear.

Oh, some as soon would throw it all
As throw a part away.
And some will say all sorts of things,
But some mean what they say.

QUESTIONING FACES

The winter owl banked just in time to pass
And save herself from breaking window glass.
And her wings straining suddenly aspread
Caught color from the last of evening red
In a display of underdown and quill
To glassed-in children at the window sill.

OUR DOOM TO BLOOM

"Shine, perishing republic."

ROBINSON JEFFERS

Cumaean Sibyl, charming Ogress,
What are the simple facts of Progress
That I may trade on with reliance
In consultation with my clients?
The Sibyl said, "Go back to Rome
And tell your clientele at home
That if it's not a mere illusion
All there is to it is diffusion—
Of coats, oats, votes, to all mankind.
In the Surviving Book we find
That liberal, or conservative,
The state's one function is to give.
The bud must bloom till blowsy blown
Its petals loosen and are strown;
And that's a fate it can't evade
Unless 'twould rather wilt than fade."

LINES WRITTEN IN DEJECTION
ON THE EVE OF GREAT SUCCESS

I once had a cow that jumped over the moon,
Not on to the moon but over.
I don't know what made her so lunar a loon;

Lines Written in Dejection on the Eve of Great Success

All she'd been having was clover.

That was back in the days of my godmother Goose.
But though we are goosier now,
And all tanked up with mineral juice,
We haven't caught up with my cow.

POSTSCRIPT

But if over the moon I had wanted to go
And had caught my cow by the tail,
I'll bet she'd have made a melodious low
And put her foot in the pail;

Than which there is no indignity worse.
A cow did that once to a fellow
Who rose from the milking stool with a curse
And cried, "I'll larn you to bellow."

He couldn't lay hands on a pitchfork to hit her
Or give her a stab of the tine,
So he leapt on her hairy back and bit her
Clear into her marrow spine.

No doubt she would have preferred the fork.
She let out a howl of rage
That was heard as far away as New York
And made the papers' front page.

He answered her back, "Well, who begun it?"
That's what at the end of a war
We always say—not who won it,
Or what it was foughten for.

QUANDARY

FROM IRON

TOOLS AND WEAPONS

To Ahmed S. Bokhari

Nature within her inmost self divides
To trouble men with having to take sides.

Four-room shack aspiring high
With an arm of scrawny mast
For the visions in the sky
That go blindly pouring past.
In the ear and in the eye
What you get is what to buy.
Hope you're satisfied to last.

ON BEING CHOSEN POET OF VERMONT

Breathes there a bard who isn't moved
When he finds his verse is understood
And not entirely disapproved
By his country and his neighborhood?

It takes all sorts of in and outdoor schooling
To get adapted to my kind of fooling.

In winter in the woods alone
Against the trees I go.
I mark a maple for my own
And lay the maple low.

At four o'clock I shoulder axe
And in the afterglow
I link a line of shadowy tracks
Across the tinted snow.

I see for Nature no defeat
In one tree's overthrow
Or for myself in my retreat
For yet another blow.

Index of Titles

Index of Titles

Index of Titles

Rinehart Editions